Literature, Life, and Modernity

COLUMBIA THEMES IN PHILOSOPHY, SOCIAL CRITICISM, AND THE ARTS

LITERATURE, LIFE, AND MODERNITY

Richard Eldridge

COLUMBIA UNIVERSITY PRESS NEW YORK

Columbia University Press
Publishers Since 1893
New York   Chichester, West Sussex
Copyright © 2008 Columbia University Press
All rights reserved

Library of Congress Cataloging-in-Publication Data
Eldridge, Richard Thomas, 1953–
   Literature, life, and modernity / Richard Eldridge.
      p. cm. — (Columbia themes in philosophy, social criticism, and the arts)
   Includes bibliographical references and index.
   ISBN 978-0-231-14454-4 (cloth: acid-free paper) —
   ISBN 978-0-231-51552-8 (e-book)
   1. Literature—Philosophy. 2. European literature—History and criticism.
   3. Literature and society. I. Title. II. Series.

PN49.E43   2008
801.3—dc22   2008001172

Columbia University Press books are printed on
permanent and durable acid-free paper.
This book is printed on paper with recycled content.

Printed in the United States of America
Designed by Audrey Smith

c 10 9 8 7 6 5 4 3 2 1

Not for these I raise
The song of thanks and praise;
But for those obstinate questionings
Of sense and outward things,
Fallings from us, vanishings;
Blank misgivings of a Creature
Moving about in worlds not realized,
High instincts before which our mortal Nature
Did tremble like a guilty Thing surprised:

> —WILLIAM WORDSWORTH, "Ode: Intimations of Immortality
> from Recollections of Early Childhood" (1807)

Ah! As I listened with a heart forlorn,
The pulses of my being beat anew:
And even as Life returns upon the drowned,
Life's joy rekindling roused a throng of pains—

> —SAMUEL TAYLOR COLERIDGE, "To William Wordsworth:
> Composed on the Night After His Recitation of a Poem
> on the Growth of an Individual Mind" (1807)

The poem of the mind in the act of finding
What will suffice. It has not always had
To find: the scene was set; it repeated what
Was in the script.
Then the theatre was changed
To something else. Its past was a souvenir.
It has to be living, to learn the speech of the place.
It has to face the men of the time and to meet
The women of the time. It has to think about war
And it has to find what will suffice.

> —WALLACE STEVENS, "Of Modern Poetry" (1940)

Contents

Acknowledgments

This book has been fortunate in the many circumstances that occasioned it and in the comments and conversations that contributed to its development. I am grateful to many friends, readers, and interlocutors for their good will, insights, and friendship. In conversations beginning around their editing of *The Literary Wittgenstein*, Wolfgang Huemer and John Gibson prompted me to begin thinking and writing more directly about the nature of distinctively literary achievement than I had done in the past. On one or another occasion, either in Philadelphia or in Erfurt, Germany, I talked with John, Wolfgang, or both about almost everything written in the analytic philosophy of literature in the last ten or so years. These conversations were invaluable for the direction of my work. Wolfgang then invited me to spend a semester at the University of Erfurt, where I taught a seminar on the philosophy of literature with Wolfgang present. Wolfgang visited Swarthmore nine months later, where we taught the philosophy of literature together for six weeks and I had the pleasure of hearing his lectures. In both settings, we talked several times a week about recent professional philosophical work on cognition, morality, and the uses of literature, and reflections of these conversations run continuously through this book. I also found in Erfurt extraordinarily congenial colleagues in Alex Burri, Carsten Held, Christian Beyer, Winfried Franzen, and Jan-Hendrik Heinrichs, in addition to Wolfgang Huemer. I cannot imagine a happier and more supportive environment in which to do philosophical work. In addition, Wolfgang Huemer and Alex Burri organized a conference on literature and cognition in Erfurt during my visit. I was able there to present an early version of part of chapter 4 and to enjoy the presentations of and discussions with Bernard Harrison, John Gibson, Wolfgang Huemer, Luca Pocci, Catherine Elgin, Christiane Schildknecht, Alex Burri, Gottfried Gabriel, Peter Lamarque, and Joachim Schulte. Thanks to Bettina Menke, I was able to present an early version of chapter 6 to the Faculty for General and Comparative Literature. Comments from Bettina Menke and Holt Meyer about the singularity of the exemplary work of literature and the nature of the literary experience have been much on my mind in subsequent writing and rewriting, and Bettina Menke helpfully corrected some points about Sebald. Reading Christoph Menke's account in *Die Souveränität der Kunst* of Kafka's literary achievement together with a subsequent conversation with him in Erfurt about this account also substantially shaped my thinking.

A yet earlier version of chapter 6 was presented at a seminar on Philosophy and Literature, sponsored by the Philosophical Society of Finland and organized by Martha Nussbaum. There I was also fortunate to be able to talk about subject development with Jonathan Lear and about romanticism and modernity with Josef Früchtl. This earlier version subsequently appeared in *Visions of Value and Truth: Understanding Philosophy and Literature*, ed. Floora Ruokonen and Laura Werner (Helsinki: The Philosophical Society of Finland, 2006), 13–29.

A somewhat later version was then presented as a lecture to the philosophy department of Purchase College of the State University of New York, where during both a wonderful general discussion and dinner I learned from and was encouraged by Casey Haskins, Morris Kaplan, Jennie Uleman, and Frank Ferrell.

Nikolas Kompridis invited chapter 3 for his volume *Philosophical Romanticism* (London: Routledge, 2006), 97–112, and I was able to present an early draft of this chapter at a meeting of the International Conference on Romanticism, where I profited from conversations with Larry Peer, Diane Hoeveler, William Davis, Eugene Stelzig, and Joshua Wilner.

Fred Rush invited me to deliver a lecture on "Romanticism and

Tom Stoppard" in a symposium for the inauguration of the DeBarto-
lo Performing Arts Center at Notre Dame. This lecture subsequently
became chapter 2, improved by the comments at Notre Dame of
Fred Rush, Charles Larmore, and Neil Delaney. A slightly later version of this chapter was delivered as a lecture to the German Society
for Aesthetics, to which I was invited by Josef Früchtl and where I received useful comments from Georg Bertram, David Lauer, and Ian
Kaplow, in addition to Josef Früchtl. A portion of this chapter will
be forthcoming in *Zeitschrift für Aesthetik und Allgemeine Kunst-
wissenschaft*, vol. 1, 2008.

Ross Wilson invited what became chapter 4 for a forthcoming volume on romantic conceptions of life. He provided acute comments
on an early draft.

A version of chapter 5 was presented as a Faculty Lecture at
Swarthmore College, where I am grateful to Alfred Bloom, Peter
Schmidt, and Robin Wagner-Pacifici for encouraging and useful re-
marks. Philip M. Weinstein subsequently read this chapter and pro-
vided written comments that not only improved it but also substan-
tially prompted and contributed to some points in the introduction.
A version of it has been published in *A Sense of the World*, ed. John
Gibson, Wolfgang Huemer, and Luca Pocci (London: Routledge,
2007), and in German in *Kunst denken*, ed. Wolfgang Huemer and
Alex Burri (Paderborn: Mentis, 2007).

During the last year or so of the writing and revising of this manuscript, I was fortunate to have been editing *The Oxford Handbook
of Philosophy and Literature*. Essays from contributors would arrive every three weeks or so for my comments. As a result, I was
continually thinking about the arguments put forward by these
contributors and comparing them with my own lines of thinking.
Without exception, I was stimulated and encouraged by essay after essay. I am aware of specific turns of thought on my part being prompted by essays by Charles Altieri, J. M. Bernstein, Simona
Bertacco, Anthony J. Cascardi, Ted Cohen, John Gibson, Bernard
Harrison, Toril Moi, Kirk Pillow, Fred Rush, Susan Stewart, and
Philip Weinstein.

Hannah Eldridge and Sarah Eldridge both attended the Erfurt conference on literature and cognition, and they have each talked regularly with me about Sebald, Rilke, Benjamin, Hegel, and romanticism, among many other topics. Each of them read drafts of sections of various chapters, and their responses were important to increasing my confidence in the coherence and direction of my argument.

Adam Haslett read a demipenultimate and then a penultimate version of the introduction. His acute comments prompted a significant structural revision and helped me to tighten the development of the argument and to make it more accessible to more readers than it might otherwise have been.

Lydia Goehr and Gregg Horowitz each read a complete, penultimate draft of the book. They offered detailed and insightful comments, criticisms, and suggestions, all of which prompted significant revisions and additions, particularly to the introduction and to chapter 6, but also throughout the manuscript as a whole. Acute comments from readers for Columbia University Press led to further productive final revisions.

Joan Vandegrift likewise read a complete, penultimate draft, and her comments led to some significant rearrangement of materials from chapter 5 to the introduction. In this, as in everything else, her ear and sense of development proved vital to the whole.

Literature, Life, and Modernity

1.

Introduction

Subjectivity, Modernity, and the Uses of Literature

The term "literature" has a fairly wide range of reasonable uses. One can talk of the literature on x—ladybugs or chess or cello varnishes, as may be—and mean only all or much of what has been written about a particular subject. In German-language scholarship, one often begins an essay with a *Literaturverzeichnis*, a review of the most important prior work on a topic, whatever the topic might be. *Children's literature* refers to books specially written for children to enjoy. These uses, however, are surely not what the Nobel or Booker Prize committees have in mind in awarding prizes for literature, nor are they what is suggested by the commendatory adjective "literary," as in "a literary person" or "of literary merit"; nor do they figure in the senses of *English literature* or *Francophone literature* as names for disciplines of study within a university curriculum.

Even where what is in view under the heading of the literary is some sort of value, there are nonetheless many different valuable experiences that literature affords. These include, among others, entertainment, consolation, the pleasures of archaic regression (reminiscent of being read to as a child), the acquisition of historical knowledge, the sharpening of personal or political hope, and absorption in and admiration of verbal virtuosity. It would be a mistake either to overlook or to underrate the considerable variety of uses that works rightly classed as literary can and do invite and support.[1]

Despite this variety of uses, however, there persists for many people a sense that literature, at least sometimes, has a central and distinctive way of mattering for human life. Such a sense supports the existence of special curricula of literary study, including the cultivation of habits of close reading, as these habits have developed with increasing, multiple specificities from the late eighteenth century to the present. Both literary scholars and many ordinary people now read novels, short stories, films, lyrics, plays, television programs, and advertising, among other things, with habits of attention to form, diction, imagery, ideology, materiality, use, and much more. Yet it is not always clear exactly what close reading discerns, nor is it clear why one should bother to read certain works closely, rather than doing the many other things there are to do in life. Somehow— or so many people think—a life would be less rich or less informed by sympathetic understanding without engagement with a specifically literary curriculum or with habits of close reading. But exactly how might this be so, if it is so at all? The undoubted existence of some persons of refined literary experience and sensibility but with little moral discernment or responsiveness shows that reading literature is not by itself sufficient to produce moral understanding. Conversations with actual people—parents, friends, neighbors, and so on—is in most cases far more important than reading in the shaping of character. Could reading some literary works nonetheless help to shape character in valuable ways? Perhaps, but then many literary works are fictions, so that there is no actual person with whom one can immediately sympathize, and some people who read literature intensively may use it mostly as a compensation for the pains of life or as a distraction from them. Might it not be easier and more reliable to learn sympathy by talking at length with wide varieties of people? Is reading literature only a shortcut for that?[2] And if it is, then why not read memoirs, history, and journalism instead? Why all that fiction? And if sympathizing with actual persons is the aim ultimately in view, then what is the significance of the specific verbal densities and formal structures of exemplary literary texts? Why are many of them so difficult, and why, if at all, does that matter?

If there is any hope of articulating plausible and useful answers to these questions, then the hard question of what a human life as such is all about will have to be faced. If human lives have no common structure and directions of achievement but instead aim at only whatever individuals, in interaction with possibilities afforded by their cultural settings, arbitrarily undertake to pursue, then literature and literary curricula will have no distinctive places in the cultivation of human life as such, for there will be nothing significantly shared to cultivate.

During the past two hundred to four hundred years in Europe and the Americas, common projects and senses of purpose were largely sufficiently established by common national language, culture, and material situation to make national literatures matter to many, at least within certain educated circles. However, in an era of increasingly global commodity markets, national and linguistic barriers become more permeable, competitive individualism and reactive fundamentalism increase, and the salience of national literatures as forms of reflection on common cultural life diminishes, as cultural life spreads out and diversifies.[3] Common and overlapping projects give way to various forms of getting, spending, enjoying, and entertaining, supported by technological advancements, unless those should turn out to be self-defeating or subjectively undesirable. As a result, factionalism increasingly displaces any sense of a political commonwealth, and culture becomes often a matter more of multiple fluid and commodified styles than a stable source of significance. Yet there is little chance of simply returning to older sureties. In a modern social world with a highly complex division of labor and with the distinctive satisfactions that attach to different social roles, religious commitments of any kind may seem either pale, abstract, and empty (churches open to all shoppers) or tyrannical and self-consciously sectarian (closing the doors to all but the pure). Either competitive individualism or competitive factionalism comes to the fore, and chances of learning to live out a common humanity with more depth become increasingly attenuated. And yet it can seem in some moments of reading that certain literary works offer us some access to increased reflective depth without dogma or tyranny. How might this be so? Can this sense in any way be trusted? And might literature help to open up some senses of possible common purpose and some routes of possible mutual engagement, hesitantly and nondogmatically, without either denying or undertaking to rule over the complexities of modern social life?

In his valuable recent study *Why Does Literature Matter?*, Frank Farrell takes up these questions, arguing that literary works function for human subjects as vehicles of partial and provisional recoveries of meaningfulness. Modern subjects, Farrell argues, suffer various kinds of loss in the courses of their developments. Thick, premodern social rituals are displaced in social space by economic transactions according to mysterious equivalences. The magical and metaphorical languages and ways of thinking that figure significantly in childhood experiences and in premodern cultures are displaced by analytical, grammatical, and scientific casts of mind and thought. Engagements with significances that are widely felt according to "the way things are done" are supplanted by individuals going opaquely about their mysterious "private" businesses.[4] For these various losses of felt significances, "the space of writing," Farrell argues, "offers us a modest compensation."[5]

The compensations that literature affords occur, according to Farrell, in various registers.[6] Phenomenologically, experience itself, for example, of a landscape or of the face and bearing of another person, is recorded in and recovered through the literary text as meaningful, rather than being left either as a source of mere "sensations" or data or being submitted to automatic, preformed categorizations. Metaphors and other devices of figuration are used to achieve and express psychic investment in and attention to what is being presented. Metaphysically, mood as an overall style or color of engagement with a natural and social world is registered, and some engagements and moods are registered as more truthful than others. Psychologically, a childhood sense of self as being caught up, fuguelike, in mysterious, larger processes of development is posed against a too assured, too rounded sense of accomplished mastery of discourses and social roles. Archaic but not quite lost rituals and senses of place are recovered or refigured. And there are the compensations of "style . . .as a staging of the psyche,"[7] with richer and more satisfying investments than are ready to hand in daily life. Overall, "we seem to have the language of literature as a necessarily repeated, even obsessive, reworking of that transitional space"[8] between the prelinguistic and the linguistic, childhood and maturity, the premodern and the modern, the metaphorical and the literal. Its modest compensations for loss challenge punctual, individual hubris and open up routes of richer attention and engagement.

Farrell has here located the function of literature against a compelling background story of how subject development is marked by the loss of various kinds of richness and intensity (experiential, premodern, ritual-archaic, fuguelike repetitive, etc.). His idea that literature works to recuperate these losses has much to recommend it. At the same time, however, it is possible to wonder how stable and assertational about human life the recuperations that literature offers finally are. Farrell himself calls them modest, as though to mark their difference from stable discovery of standing sources of sharable felt significance in life. When the recuperative and instructive powers of literature are emphasized, then both its powers to disrupt and its failures to arrive at conclusive doctrinal closure are underplayed.

David Wellbery usefully registers literature's disruptive force and formal distinctiveness as he describes the "problematic and uncertain representational, or perhaps epistemological status"[9] of certain poems and, by implication, of exemplary literature in general. Wellbery develops his conception of the literary as a site of formed disruption through commenting on Goethe's lyric "Wilkommen und Abschied"—a lyric that on a narrative-thematic level describes the achievement of bliss. The concluding couplet of "Wilkommen" represents and summarizes an outburst of bliss that is grounded in an experience of the gaze of the beloved. "Und doch, welch Glück! Geliebt zu werden. / Und lieben, Götter, welch ein Glück [And yet, what bliss!, to be loved, / And to love, you gods! What bliss!]."[10] Within the very structure of its formulation, however, this outburst reveals itself as artfully and rhetorically achieved, not simply the spontaneous, naïve, and accessibly inimitable product of immediate passion. As Wellbery puts it, "the chiastic structure 'Glück . . .-lieb // lieb- Glück' and the passive-active reversal of the verb . . .*constitute a structural emblem for the entire poem*."[11] That is, the concluding lines ("lieb- Glück") embody an inversion, both thematic-semantic and phonological-formal, of material that has been used earlier in the poem, so that this "closing formulation proves to be in many respects a recapitulation within a reduced format of the essential features of lines 25–30."[12] Through this use of semantic and formal figuration, repetition, and condensation, the poem is marked as literary and achieves its end. It achieves aesthetic closure in historically specific ways, and it disrupts simpler communicative assertion of independent facts. It invites absorption in its artifices as much or more than proposing any recommendations for individual or social recuperation. Disruption and absorption in formal achievement significantly displace any moment of theoretical-instrumental instruction, individual or social. On the larger historical-thematic level, moreover, "Wilkommen" figures the gaze of an individual beloved rather than, say, either the presence of God or involvement in ritual as the source of bliss. Thus the poem is marked as a more or less modern work that, in using its theme, carries "inadvertent traces and remainders of cultural production."[13] Once upon a time, that is, things were otherwise: bliss was either figured as having other sources or was not so intensively pursued by subjects who were less inward and more clan-immersed and either epic-heroic or immiserated than the modern, individual speaking persona of "Wilkommen."

So it is, always, with exemplary literature. The most successful writers use both thematic materials and devices of figuration that are in some measure historically specific. They use these materials and devices self-consciously to register and attend to a moment of crisis or loss in an individual, within a culture, or between cultures. They manage to represent this crisis fully, avoiding repression and cliché,

and avoiding also resolution according to the terms of any philosophical or religious doctrine of value. Yet they manage to achieve,
in and through the interaction of thematic materials with formal devices that mark the work as literary, densities and closures that com-
pel their readers—or those among their readers who share enough of
their losses and crises—to become absorbed in them, to follow their
self-sustaining work, without taking away any formulable-assertible
message about reality outside the work. Hence the terms of the modest compensations that literature offers are simultaneously thematic
in relation to specific historical materials and formal-aesthetic-dis-
ruptive-autonomous. There is no single path, smooth and bright, for
either the achievement of literary value or its transportation into the
rest of life. The occasions of crisis and loss that provoke literary attention are too various for that, ungoverned by any superintending
historical logic, and the use of figures as devices of attention is likewise both historically marked and bound to specific thematic historical materials. Yet somehow, nonetheless, exemplary writers come to
terms in exemplary ways with a kind of permanent human immigrancy or fracturedness, with what Eric Santner has characterized as
"the *signifying stress* at the core of creaturely life."[14] Human beings
in their courses of development are able sometimes to give voice to
the situations of crisis and loss that mark their lives as subjects of
and within culture, capable of awareness of their situations. They
can attend to and work through the stresses, both individual and cultural, that mark their lives. But the work they accomplish is less the
work of arriving at a doctrine than it is, in Heideggerian terms, the
working of the work itself: its having its way of bringing together its
thematic materials and figural-rhetorical devices to embody a fullness of attention coupled with a satisfaction in the forming of the
work in which its readers may share (or may not).

Within modernity, the stresses that force themselves into consciousness—stresses to which the work of art then responds—come
increasingly from the late eighteenth century on to involve conflict
between the claims of the sensible (what we discern and attach ourselves to through embodied feeling) and the intelligible (what we

discern and attach ourselves to via distantiation and the controlled measurement of what there is). Claims of intimacy, solidarity, and cathexis to daily routine jostle against claims to knowledge, objectivity, and clear-sightedness about what there "at bottom" "really" is. Feeling is itself internalized, by being cast as something "subjective" with measurable intensities and durations, and its claims to being a mode of responsive knowledge are challenged. Whatever any individual happens to like or dislike becomes a matter only of more or less measurable fact (perhaps as a revealed preference, perhaps something one can report about oneself); what emotion, feeling, and mood discern as worth responding to or being involved with fades in cognitive power. Our work, our intimate relations, and our political citizenship, among other things, become matters, at best, of private satisfactions, troubled by the fact or threat that the private satisfactions of tomorrow may displace them, as either the menus of options or one's own whims change. Stability, depth, and lived meaningfulness founder. As J. M. Bernstein puts it: "The most profound challenge to the unity and unifying work of [modern] culture is the separation, diremption, gap, or abyss separating the sensible world we aspire to live in every day, the world of things known through sight and sound and touch and feel, from the exactitudes of scientific explanation."[15] Unsupported by a sense that they are rooted in any accurate discernment of how things are, "our moods do not believe in each other,"[16] and we drift, perhaps seeking medication to dull anxiety and depression.

One way to begin to address the problems of drift and of the disruption of cathexis is to see the modern work of art as occupying "a strange place at the intersection of the axes of the actual and eternal,"[17] as Jürgen Habermas usefully characterizes Baudelaire's conception of the artwork. According to this conception, the authentic modern work of art "is radically bound to the moment of its emergence; precisely because it consumes itself in actuality, it can bring the steady flow of trivialities to a standstill, break through normality, and satisfy for a moment the immortal longing for beauty—a moment in which the eternal comes into fleeting contact with the actual."[18]

It is, however, not so easy to say what the eternal's coming into fleeting contact with the actual amounts to. Baudelaire himself speaks of "eternal and invariable . . .Beauty" taking on an "amusing, teasing, appetite-whetting coating"[19] from circumstantial actuality. Whatever the "shining forth" of the eternal within the coating of the actual may involve, however, it evidently does not involve accession on the part of the audience to any guiding doctrine or articulated sense of where beyond the work meaningfulness is to be found. Aesthetic absorption in the work overwhelms any moment of instruction. Where, as in the novel, more generalized reflections on meaningfulness sometimes appear, writers are continually forced to exercise powers of construction and of the making of meaning against the grain of an actuality that significantly involves the merely happenstantial. Fates experienced as meaningful—certain exemplary marriages or deaths, say—are as much the inventions of modern writers as they are found ready-made in modern life. As long as it avoids cliché and sustains attention to life, the modern novel, along with modern art in general, suffers from what Georg Lukács calls a characteristic "normative incompleteness": it cannot say what is to be done. In Bernstein's similar perception, "at its highest reach, [modern] art turns cultural melancholy into form."[20] The work invites and sustains absorption in it, in the face of the pains of modern life, and within the work complexities and unresolved resistances come increasingly to displace meaningful closures.

Historically, modern and modernist literary texts present dramas of heroic individual resistance against decayed or opaque social formations. The forms of resistance may range from Quixote's comic fancies to Hamlet's tragic uncertainties to the compressed intensities of the lyrics of Goethe or Keats, among many others. Trauma and failure of fully stable and meaningful subject formation are registered in tragic losses, comic flights, or asides of lyric ecstasy. Sometimes a good enough resolution is found for a few, against the grain of the prevailing social order, though in chastened awareness of its presence, as in Jane Austen. Good enough resolutions become, perhaps, less available in more characteristically modernist as opposed to modern texts.[21] More "postmodern" texts use devices of collage, juxtaposition, and intertextuality (satire and allusion, especially across genres and between popular and "high" culture) in order to emphasize the inabilities of cultures or individuals to settle on specific, clear, final narrative arcs. Positions, ideologies, cultures, and points of view collide with one another all but endlessly. It is impossible, however, to distinguish in sharp and absolute terms modern-modernist dramas of individual crisis (partially resolved or not) from postmodernist anarchic collage and juxtaposition. Where, for example, would one place *Tristram Shandy*? Is *Gravity's Rainbow* not in part a drama of individual crisis? When they achieve exemplarity, literary texts present both dramas of crisis and moments of sheer contingency. Hence in either form—relatively modern-modernist or relatively postmodern—what modern literature knows is that no comprehensive resolution of crises within individual or social development is possible: some satisfaction must be found within the working of the work itself, as a kind of placeholder for what is never finally achieved. Human beings, at least within the orbit of a modern individualism that remains powerfully with us, persist as caught up in signifying stresses arising out of a sense of slippage of "inner," passionate, embodied, archaic selfhood away from "outer," articulated, social role and agency.[22] In modernity, such slippage is inevitable, and the task of literature is more to figure its forms than to propose standing resolutions.

There are, in all likelihood, deep reasons for this kind of literary practice, deep reasons that suggest that literature's registerings of human finitude and the impossibility of specifically legislative moral knowledge are apt to human life as such. Human consciousness is marked by intentionality. That is, human beings not only represent their environments to themselves through perception, they are also aware of their own representings. They can "intend" objects that are not materially present (golden mountains, centaurs, time-travel machines, and the like) and they can imagine themselves perceiving and acting in counterfactual situations with much greater range, depth, and flexibility than can other animals.

Hence for human beings questions of correctness in judgment can arise explicitly. "Am I," we are capable of asking, "correct to judge that this is a stick or a weapon or a digging implement or firewood (or all four)? Or am I rather imagining a context of use that is either not ready to hand or not shared by others? Just what am I doing when I am judging that things are thus-and-so, and am I here and now right or not?" Other sensate and conscious creatures do not display this kind of plasticity of attention, self-awareness, and engagement with questions of correctness.

As philosophers as different from one another as Aristotle, Hegel, Dewey, Wittgenstein, and Adorno have argued, this combination of plasticity of attention, self-awareness, and involvement with normativity is not a purely material phenomenon, even though it has a necessary material basis. This thought is further supported by the detailed ethnographic observations of childhood language learning carried out by Michael Tomasello.[23] Instead of being wholly determined by biological-material processes alone, conceptual consciousness begins in training and mimicry, in learning within contexts of joint attention to see *this* (this stick, this wooden object, this whatever it is) *as this or that* (as a stick, a weapon, a digging implement, firewood, etc.) The emergence of self-awareness and the emergence of involvement with normativity are coeval with the emergence of conceptual consciousness. ("Am I right to see this as that? How do others see it? Am I doing what is wanted of me in picking up this stick, this ball, this penny [as the child learns later to call them]?") Is there a proof from contact with ultimate givens that conceptual consciousness, self-awareness, and involvement with normativity thus emerge? No. But try to explain its emergence either metaphysically or purely materially: all the familiar problems of the ineliminability of normativity and responsibility arise. (Do we live in order to represent or represent in order to live?)

Because, however, human beings are capable of plastic attention and face widely divergent and ever-changing problem situations, multiple patterns of engagement with objects under concepts are always available, and these patterns of engagement (conceptual repertoires) change and are contested. The dream of rooting perfect and unchallengeable conceptual consciousness, freed of all critical

engagement with normativity, in ecstatic, intuitive contact with ultimate givens (Platonic forms, sempiternal atoms) is haunting but
idle.[24] Training in contexts of mutual attention that are open to contestation cannot be overleaped. Meaning—what things are for in relation to contexts of use, what courses of action are fulfilling in what
ways—is not to be discovered in anything simply given in the absence
of circuits of training and imitation. "There will not be books in the
running brooks until the dawn of hydro-semantics"[25]—and hydro-
semantics shows no sign of dawning.

The idea that we bear a continuing responsibility for and continuing anxieties about our lives as conceptually conscious subjects who
are caught up in patterns of attention that are subject to contestation
is originally and most powerfully formulated by Kant. Kant's philosophical anthropology is rooted in a sense of human life as having
two aspects or dimensions. (Human reason has this peculiar, divided
fate.) First, we are beings who possess apperceptive awareness or
self-consciousness; that is, we are beings who are at least implicitly
and potentially aware of our judgments and actions as our own. We
further possess the power to become more explicitly aware of our
judgments and actions as our own and to raise questions about their
correctness: to submit them to critical reflection in the pursuit of
greater reasonableness, fluency, stability of character, and human
command. Second, we are finite beings who exist within nature and
culture and who are unable to refer that existence to any ultimate
grounding. Within both nature and culture, there is the possibility
always of surprise, of a discovery of one's own itinerancy, and of being
at this moment out of attunement with nature, culture, and oneself.

The fact that we possess both these senses of ourselves is brought
powerfully into awareness by the experience of modernity. That Kant
expresses both senses is what makes him, along with Descartes, a
modern, even modernist, philosopher. Descartes proposes that "a
good man has no need to have read every book, nor to have carefully
learned all that which is taught in the schools; it would even be a
defect in his education were he to have devoted too much time to the
study of letters."[26] Thus he sets his face as a freethinking individual

against the authority of culture as it stands, seeking a new form of the purely rational expression of purely individual rational powers in the practice of modern mathematical-experimental science. We must, as Kant will later put it, "dare to know,"[27] against the grain of the culturally given.

Descartes' confidence in the availability and value of this new form of practice is underwritten officially by his initial certainty of his own existence, coupled with his subsequent a priori arguments for the existence of God and for God's having made physical nature such that we can know it by doing the right kind of science. But one can also, if one listens closely, hear an undercurrent of anxiety in Descartes' formulations.[28] "'I am, I exist' is necessarily true each time that I pronounce it, or that I mentally conceive it."[29] But what if I fail to do this, fail to pronounce my own existence, perhaps out of timidity in the exercise of my rational powers, or perhaps because I am more caught up than I suppose in the culture that does not embody fully human, rational life, or perhaps because nature in the end will not fully support the exercise of rational powers? Do I then fail to exist necessarily? "I am, I exist, that is certain. But how often? Just when I think; for it might possibly be the case if I ceased entirely to think, that I should likewise cease altogether to exist."[30] Coupled with the thoughts that the mass of humanity has more or less continuously failed to think fully or clearly and that nature is not intuitively or immediately knowable, this form of self-certainty is not exactly a recipe for confidence in life, even if the practices of modern science turn out to be comparatively fruitful and cognitively satisfying. The power to reflect on one's judgments and actions has here established a certain distance from ultimate grounding in either metaphysical givens or mere naturalness, no matter what assurances follow and no matter what the successes of modern science are. And is it clear that we either can or should forego wide-ranging reflectiveness? There is, in Stanley Cavell's terms, a kind of standing "nextness of the self to the self."[31] As Thoreau puts it, "I am conscious of the presence and criticism of a part of me, which, as it were, is not a part of me, but a spectator, sharing no experience, but taking note of it, and that is no more I than it is you."[32] Hence, in Cavell's gloss, the self bears, always, two attitudes toward itself, as it finds "that it is the watchman or guardian of itself, and hence demands of itself transparence, settling, clearing, consistency; and that it is the workman, whose eye cannot see to the end of its labors, but whose answerability is endless for the constructions in which it houses itself."[33] (If one can hear an inflection of class in the distinction between superintending watchman and laboring workman, one should also remember that, as in Hegel, it is the workman to whom any future belongs.) Our freely formed commitments are entangled in and yet outrun reflectiveness—a sense of self that while perhaps always existentially given also becomes especially prominent in modernity, as possible directions of commitment multiply and sheer immersion in necessities of survival diminishes somewhat.

Kant then widens, sharpens, and literalizes a modern, Cartesian sense of the possibility and value of awakening through reflectiveness into new and better commitments, coupled with a sense of lingering anxieties and uncertainties. We have, always, according to Kant, apperceptive awareness of the possibility of noting and reflecting on our commitments as our own. While we are bound by the categorical imperative as a law of pure practical reason or reflective deliberation in abstraction from inclinations and desires (and what is that?), we know neither how or why this is so nor what the proper specific directions of response to our being so bound must be (even if certain prohibitions are clear). Nature "reveals little, but very little"[34] of a path toward a kingdom of ends. "Man must give [the] autocracy of the soul its full scope; otherwise he becomes a mere plaything of other forces and impressions which withstand his will, and a prey to the caprice of accident and circumstance."[35] But how? And, especially, how over time, continuously, in relation to others and to the changing affordances of culture? We seem to bear, always, and especially in modernity, senses of ourselves as both capable of reflection and cast in courses of life we cannot wholly survey.

To the extent, then, that these senses of ourselves can be reconciled, that reconciliation will take the form of the expression in judgment and action of an increased (but not perfect) sense of reasonableness, fluency, character, and command mixed with a sense of finitude, apartness, and contingency. This reconciliation will always be partial and provisional. It is not circumscribable according to any fixed policy or order of conceptualization. (Claims to such a circumscription would transgress standing human finitude.) Instead, it is best conceived of as a kind of temporarily displayed power, roughly what Kant calls *Mündigkeit*, or maturity. ("Enlightenment is man's release from his self-incurred tutelage [*Unmündigkeit*].")[36] The implied metaphor in *Mündigkeit* (*Mund* = mouth) of coming to speech or voice is apt. We are able to achieve, and we are to achieve, not final moral knowledge but rather a certain kind of more fluent, clearer, more formed, more focused, and more articulate stance or address to or in life. As Thomas Pfau remarks in commenting on the use of "voice" (*Stimme*) and associated terms such as mood, attunement, determination, and agreement (*Stimmung, Bestimmung, Übereinstimmung*) in the *Critique of Judgment*, Kant's conception of voice is understandable as "aiming to reconcile, however provisionally, the experience of a deeply significant interiority with an articulation of its social significance" in a way that "manifests a unique form of desire"[37]—a desire for fluently expressive, reasonable self-command in judgment and action within social space: a desire for recognition, which desire does not admit of perfect satisfaction.

Our efforts to move toward increased fluency, clarity, and command begin not simply in a grasp of abstract universals, not simply in the law-governed motions of physical particles, and not simply in our psychological hardwiring but also in and through following, imitating, and reacting to the subjectivities of others, as manifested in directions of gaze and interest. Aristotle captures this point in remarking that human beings, in contrast with other animals, are "thoroughly mimetic and through mimesis take [their] first steps in understanding."[38] Others use words of some generality and potential for use on further occasions; in doing so they manifest certain directions of gaze and interest. They manage their uses in virtue of having mastered prevailing routines well enough. But their masteries and the uses that flow from them remain ungrounded in any ultimate realities. Hence at least some uses are liable and likely to shift over time as routes of interest and feeling shift. To come to conceptualization through the mimesis of specific routes of usage, gaze, and interest is to be caught up in a stable enough but also pluralized and partially contested life of subjectivity in the world. There may be good reason to regard certain kinds as "really instanced" in nature. There is no good reason to suppose that water or tigers, say, are arbitrary human constructs, and this situation is unlikely to change. But this stable situation does not root the life of concepts "in" nature alone, independently of mimetic circuits.

Mastery and fluency within a life with concepts are hence to be understood not simply as a grasp of fixed archetypes, patterns, or *Bedeutungskörper* that lie "behind" usage in a standing way, but rather as matters of a grasp of patterns together with an ability both to imitate and to redirect gaze and interest—to respond anew to life. Only when we see that conceptualization involves all this can we arrive at a form of philosophical understanding that is not blind to the life of human subjectivity in its life with words. Adorno makes this point eloquently in recommending "extinguishing the autarky of the concept," that is, recommending that we see both the possession and the very nature of concepts as bound up with stable enough but also sometimes contestable mimetic circuits rather than rooted in "contact" with absolute givens.

> A philosophy that . . . extinguishes the autarky of the concept strips the blindfold from our eyes. . . . Insight into the constitutive character of the nonconceptual [i.e., the deictic, sensuous, and mimetic] in the concept would end the compulsive identification which the concept brings unless halted by such reflection. Reflection upon its own meaning is the way out of the concept's seeming being-in-itself as a unit of meaning.[39]

Only this recognition of the nature of the concept—the beginning and partial continuance of the life of concepts in mimesis, where there are always residues, remainders, and other possibilities—blocks philosophy from dehistoricized, potentially smug policymongering and permits a grasp of life. "Disenchantment of the concept is the antidote of philosophy. It keeps it from growing rampant and becoming an absolute to itself."[40]

Here "disenchantment of the concept" and "the antidote of philosophy" might well be taken as significations for literature and its work. Literature foregrounds reconfigurative responsiveness to incidents and actions that take place in time over static depiction of the physically objectual, and it foregrounds figuration and the expression of attitude and emotion toward what is depicted over measurement and neutral classification. But literature is also a form of thinking that uses concepts in order to seek orientation in life under forms of emplotment and in order to work through perplexity. Conceptual identity thinking and mimesis, thought and emotion, recognition and pleasure in form, philosophy and literature—the members of these pairs are all essentially interrelated, as human beings take their first steps in understanding (toward conceptualization) through mimetic responsiveness in practice and then continue to seek more fluent, stable orientation in their lives in time. Working against conceptual ossification and taking seriously perplexities and failures of orientation that demand address, literature undertakes to reconfigure patterns of mimesis so as to embody freer and fuller responsiveness, in order to form more whole and stable individuals, forms of culture, and conceptual repertoires. "The trace of memory in mimesis, which every artwork seeks, is simultaneously always the anticipation of a condition beyond the diremption of the individual and the collective."[41] "Always the anticipation"—diremption, within individuals and between individual and collective, is never wholly overcome. There is no arrival at complete, detailed, specific understanding of shared, coherent institutions and practices and at satisfaction within them, no coming to fulfillment of any Hegelian idea of freedom. But greater fullness of orientation, resolution of perplexity, and clarity and adequacy of feeling remain possible, and literature remains, always (along with other forms of art, but with its own special verbal achievements and sense of temporality), a central form of the pursuit of these possibilities.

Put somewhat more domestically, the thought is that literature helps us to engage anew—more reasonably, with more wholeheartedness and fullness of attention and less incoherence—with life. As Catherine Wilson puts it,

> A person may learn from a novel [or other work of literature] . . . if he is forced to revise or modify, e.g. his concept of "reasonable action" through recognition of an alternative as presented in the novel [or other work]. . . . The term learning applies [here] primarily to a modification of a person's concepts, which is in turn capable of altering his thought or conduct, and not primarily to an increased disposition to utter factually correct statements or to display technical prowess. . . . The ability to go beyond what has actually been fed in in the teaching process stems . . . from a more fundamental—and perhaps even radical—alteration in the way in which he perceives [certain phenomena of life].[42]

To these claims it needs to be added only that the occasion for literary writing and for responsive literary reading is typically perplexity in life or something not making emotional or narratable sense; that the modification of concepts involves also the modification of emotion, stance, and action; that the aim is increased fluency, clarity, coherence, and felt aptness of orientation within life in culture; and that the occasions for modification are endless.

Pressure is placed on our concepts, stances, and attitudes as they stand by perplexities—in large cases by traumas—that those concepts, stances, and attitudes do not readily accommodate. By taking up literary work as either a writer or a reader, one may respond fruitfully to such pressure in a variety of ways. Sometimes one may successfully work through a perplexity or trauma so as to arrive at a fuller, more emotionally and attitudinally apt stance and story about what is going on. Perplexities of emotional entanglement and of stance can sometimes be resolved in the achievement of a kind of more stable and apt calm, in a way that Spinoza describes in his *Ethics*. Or sometimes one can (also) become more actively engaged in and satisfied within the sheer activity of either making or following a literary form as an expression of alert and masterful subjectivity, as Charles Altieri has suggested, in tracking what he calls the particulars of rapture that writers sometimes achieve and in which readers sometimes share.[43] Or sometimes one can (also) modify one's courses of action in life, so as to embody more fully both more resolved stances and more accomplished energies of form-making. Always the work of the formation and enactment of subjecthood and culture remains unfinished, remains to be done anew.

If that work remains always unfinished, one might nonetheless hope to elucidate it (rather than to master and explain it by reference to fixed externalities) by setting various exemplary pieces of that work in comparison and contrast with each other. Instead of subsuming all cases of the work of literature under a master universal or Platonic form, one might see some cases as forming what Wittgenstein calls a perspicuous representation (*übersichtliche Darstellung*), an arrangement of cases that enables "just that understanding which consists in 'seeing connexions.'"[44] One can, or at least one can hope that one can, come to see how subjectivity begins its life within intersubjective, mimetic relations and thence seeks orientation within that life in a variety of ways via literary attention, with different achievements of composure, focus of attention, and deployment of energy. A particular arrangement of such cases will be, at least when it is successful, a "*Darstellung der Darstellungen*"[45]—a figured, materially specific presentation of various figured, materially specific presentations of the life and work of subjectivity. Here, in the chapters that follow, a play, a novella (coupled with a philosophical self-interrogation), an extended lyric poem, an unconventional sonnet, and a long story are set in juxtaposition, together with various more generalizing materials, in the hope of constructing an elucidation of the workings of literature in relation to the lives of modern subjects.

This presentation of cases will neither erase all differences among them nor spare readers the critical work of comparing differences as well as similarities. Stoppard's recovery of the patterned ritual of dancing, for a viewing audience outside the action, is not the same as Goethe's letting go of Werther in order to continue his own life of writing. Wordsworth's ending in modest prayer and chastened hope is not the same as either Rilke's call for a turn or Sebald's witness and wonder. Notably, Stoppard and Sebald as contemporary writers seem less committed to hope and resolution, or are less able to give them articulate expression, than are Goethe and Wordsworth, as though the times were bleaker than they were one hundred or two hundred years ago. (Do our moods believe in each other less than they did around 1800? For what reasons? Are we to conclude that they are unable to believe in each other at all?) Yet there are also affinities among these cases. Relative calm and aesthetic closure are achieved, and life is seen through the work more steadily and whole, without denying complexity and conflict.

Seeing that the reading and writing of literature cultivate a kind of reflective depth, a kind of complex seeing that is achieved through figure and form, may help us then to avoid reducing literature to "anything that is written." It may further help us to find a way between the Scylla of didacticism and the Charybdis of formalism. Surely literature must "say something" about life. But surely, too, the way in which what is said matters, and literature produces less "moral news" than didacticism supposes. The suggestion, then, is that literature is a sort of formally significant attention to life, where what *shows* in literary forms of attention and arrangement of materials is a continuing aspiration for expressive freedom and fulfillment, typically both shaped and frustrated, in part, in specific ways in specific cultural settings. We see ourselves as pursuers of expressive freedom in situ, under difficult conditions, and we so see ourselves in the protagonists and authorial personae whom we encounter (or create). By thus recognizing ourselves, we can become somewhat more reflectively deep about the contours of human life in time.

In a recent book on the philosophy of art, I claim that "works of art [literary and otherwise] present a subject matter as a focus for thought and emotional attitude, distinctively fused to the imaginative exploration of material."⁴⁶ This definition of art—if that is the right word—specifies criteria in Wittgenstein's sense for the use of the word "art." It undertakes "to elucidate and organize our linguistic and conceptual practice, in a situation in which we are confused by the varieties of artistic practice, by the varieties of things people say about them, and by the powerful but obscure character of our own responses,"⁴⁷ and yet where, still, something can be said about what we do.

In relation to literature, what this means is that literature as an art, when it is successful, has representational-thematic, expressive-attitudinal, and formal-material dimensions, all in interaction with one another. This thought is in the spirit of Aristotle's claim in the *Poetics* that a successful tragic drama will be a presentation (mimesis) of an action with all of plot, character, thought, melody, diction, and spectacle. According to Aristotle, each of these parts of a successful tragic drama must be properly coordinated with the others. Too much spectacle and too little plot, for example, will yield in one way the episodic and in another way what are perhaps the excesses of Euripedean stagecraft or the special-effects movie. Too much plot and too little thought will yield a dramatic structure that lacks general thematic significance or that will fail to satisfy the requirement of presenting the universal in the particular. Too little melody, diction, and spectacle—that is, too little concern for the embodiment of the presentation in just a certain set of words and stagings, both crafted and felt—will likewise fail in presentational power or illumination, presenting instead only what is already known and distinctively clarifying nothing.

More abstractly, content and form both matter, and they matter in their specific ways of relating to one another. As Wolfgang Huemer has recently remarked, "If we try to define what is particular about literary texts, we find that they put an emphasis not on *what* is said, but on *how* it is said; literary language makes itself manifest. . . . At least to some extent in literary texts language itself becomes the topic."⁴⁸

An emphasis on *how* what is said is said is especially prominent in the so-called L = A = N = G = U = A = G = E poets, such as Charles Bernstein and Clark Coolidge, with their radicalization of both the voice of lyric poetry and the symbolistic-imagism of objectivism. Yet even they, while foregrounding the sheer look, sound, and feel of words and assonances, produce texts that admit of some paraphrasability and readability. One can—just barely—say what they are about. Hence one should say instead that literary texts put emphasis not *only* on what is said (represented and expressed) but *also* on how it is said.

Such emphases are also often in play in so-called ordinary speech and writing, in contexts from journalism to conversation to criticism to history. But this just shows that, as Huemer goes on to remark, "Literature . . . is not a niche phenomenon; it must not be viewed as an unnecessary but entertaining ornament, but rather as a practice central to our language without which we might not even be able to master a language as complex as ours in the first place."[49] The special intensities literature achieves are not sideways to life, with their own special domains of objects known such as possible worlds or fictional objects; they are rather part of specially apt attention—all at once representational-thematic, emotional-attitudinal, and craftlike-sensuous—to ordinary life. These intensities are achieved through the controlled and aptly original use of devices that structure perception, thought, and feeling, including emplotment, metaphor, allegory, irony, hyperbole, understatement, and assonance, among many, many others.

Through the apt use of such literary devices, fullness of attention (ideational, emotional, and sensuous) is achieved rather than shirked. Cliché, or unthinking repetition of what is merely rote and stock, is the enemy of literary art. The satisfaction sought in literary art involves what Spinoza called the transformation of an inadequate idea of an affection into a more adequate idea.[50] Through literary art one gains a better understanding of what is worth feeling and caring about in what ways, where this better understanding is grounded in what one does in fact feel and care about when one pays the fullest possible attention to the objects and quality of one's experience. By following the work of literary art, one may move into a structure of care, reflection, and investment in activity that is more stable and appropriate to the objects and events of human life. Such moves may also include involvement in the work itself, in its specifically formed patterns of attending, partly (but only partly) beyond the objects of attention. Literary art has its disruptive powers as well as its powers of focusing on phenomena of human life.

To be interested in literary art thus means being attentive to what William Rothman and Marian Keane have called "the astonishing capacities for meaningfulness that [works of art] have discovered within the singular conditions of their medi[a]."[51] These capacities of meaningfulness involve in literature the achievement of fullness of attention to phenomena of life through the use of literary devices. Through such fullness of attention, a structure of care, reflection, and investment in activity is achieved, so that we lead more freely and fully the lives of persons or selves who take an interest in their worlds, rather than being buffeted about by experience received only passively and inchoately. Apart from the kinds of noticings, expressings, and respondings that art and literature can embody and support, our lives can become pale, conventionalized, anonymous, or, one might say, not deep, not so fully the lives of subjects. And beyond the attention to life it affords, there is also the astonishment of the work itself, that it has found a way to mean once again or anew.

A significant corollary of this view about literature, attention, and fuller personhood is that writing and reading are understood as neighboring modes of activity, both of which involve the cultivation of attention. What we do when we read well is follow and identify with achievements of fuller attention as they are managed in situ by both writers, on the one hand, and protagonists in literary works, on the other.[52] What I am suggesting is that the life of persons inherently involves the pursuit of a fuller and more stable structure of care, reflection, and investment in activity (despite or across tragic inhibitions) in densely textured ways in specific cultural settings.

In describing the various individual cases that I take up, I am sometimes led to formulate claims about how we respond to a particular line or image, or even more broadly about what we are like. I am aware that this usage of "we" is far from common in literary studies and that there are significant reasons for being suspicious of it. Perhaps, therefore, it will be of some help to say something explicitly about exactly what kind of enterprise is implied by this usage.

"We" as I use it (and as it is typically used by philosophers of certain kinds) is meant to be improvisatory and invitational: to invite others to share in and test a thought for themselves. It is not meant to be a report on the results of research into what countable individuals have in fact said or thought or felt. Claims about how we respond, what we feel, and what we are like are, therefore, in a distinctive way vulnerable, naked, and exposed. This invitational (philosophical) usage of "we" traces back at least to Socrates, when he remarks in the *Republic* that we can be (must be) "ourselves both jury and advocates at once"[53] in considering what will count as more fulfilling conditions of human life. We may try, that is, to be clearer and more articulate about fundamental interests, in such a way that others may also share in both the process and the articulation of results—a very tentative and vulnerable enterprise indeed, and not at all declamatory. This same usage of "we" appears in ordinary language philosophy when what we say is investigated. Astonishingly, such claims about what we say can sometimes command assent of some circumference, and they can do so for those within that circumference with an air of overwhelming naturalness, reasonableness, and rightness to the ear. (J. L. Austin was a master at articulating such claims.) When this happens, a community of articulate understanding and commitment discovers itself in and through the common acceptance of such claims.

Once upon a time, perhaps in the heyday of New Criticism, poetry was read in something like this spirit, that is, with attention to "how we are moved" by the poem, how "we" follow its sense, etc. Since the end of that heyday, it has been "discovered" that not everyone either interprets or responds to a given poem (to any poem) in the same way. This is certainly true. Even the claims about what we feel or say or respond to that achieve the widest circumference will fall short of universality. There is no perfect route for the mimetic enactment of subjecthood; there are too many contending ambitions and senses of self housed within persistent cultural antagonisms for everyone to respond alike. The energy would be drained out of cultural life were that uniformity of response *per impossible* to come about. Difference neither should be nor can be so easily overleaped. As a result, however, of the "discovery" of diversity of response, the study of literature has become an increasingly sociologized enterprise. Cultural studies as a field arises out of the thought that we should study in a systematic, empirical, nondoctrinaire way who in actual fact says (and feels) what when. (Bourdieu is a paradigm of this study, and his empirical investigations of differences in cultural reception have been taken up in literary studies by figures such as John Barrell, Marjorie Levinson, Jerome McGann, and Edward Said, among many others.) That is, of course, something that can be done, and it can yield interesting and important results. It would by no means be an obvious advance to go back to the smugness and staleness of certain forms of New Criticism without having these other kinds of critical, cultural investigation also going on.

In the face of all this, why then might anyone still bother with the vain effort to articulate what we say, feel, or respond to, knowing that any such effort is doomed to partiality and so to a form of failure? The worry is that without such efforts we abandon ourselves to a modern, materialist, competitive, value-denigrating individualism that destroys all circuits of the mimesis of response and so destroys the very life of subjectivity as such. What is left without this effort is a culture of the competitively individualist seeking of the satisfaction of subjective preferences, without any sources of a commonwealth and without stability or depth of individual identity over time, but instead only pervasive cultural crassness, economic and political exploitation, and individual anomie. Hence it may be worthwhile, at least sometimes, to persist in the vain effort to form both communities of interpretation and evaluation and a more stable and fully invested life for individual subjectivity in and through the common acceptance of what we say. The effort to do this is a defining ambition for philosophy, literature, and criticism that it would be impoverishing to forego, however impossible it is to complete it. *Ich kann nicht anders.*

If we cannot productively engage in this work of the formation of deeper, subjectively fuller senses of self and of shared commitment, then we are, as subjects, lost, dead. But out of a fear of loss of culture and subjecthood in culture as it stands, one can sometimes do something. One can pay attention to what is perplexing in life (and in art) in the hope both of resolving one's emotional and attitudinal stance into something calmer and more stable and of mobilizing greater energies of commitment. One can write about one's perplexities, and one can read one's way through others' ways of encountering perplexity that are more articulate and more persuasive than one's own. And then one can, and must, wait, unable either to control the response of any audience or to form an audience of universal circumference. This is what certain writers (and other artists) have always somehow known how to do for us in detail, endlessly, with power, grace, and responsiveness to life, and in the furtherance of life.

2.

Romanticism, Cartesianism, Humeanism, Byronism

Stoppard's Arcadia

What philosophy knows as the mind-body problem is also and perhaps more deeply a problem in our practical, cultural lives and in the self-images that are woven through them. It is hard to avoid thinking of ourselves as "free subjectivities," capable of choice and responsiveness to reasons, who stand "over against" a physical nature in which objects are composed and events occur according to laws that make no reference to choices or reasons. But this makes it difficult to see how choice and responsiveness to reasons can be expressed within a "mere" nature that somehow "houses" our lives and practices. How, if at all, is free life according to reason and within the framework of the natural world possible? We shall scarcely be able to make progress on this question until we confront the cultural practices that embody and shape our images of nature and of ourselves.

John Dewey makes the practical, cultural dimensions of the mind-body problem wonderfully clear in a long passage from *Art as Experience*:

We inherit much from the cultures of the past. The influence of Greek science and philosophy, of Roman law, of religion having a Jewish source, upon our present institutions, beliefs and ways of thinking and feeling is too familiar to need more than mention. Into the operation of these factors two forces have been injected that are distinctly late in origin and that constitute the "modern" in the present epoch. These two forces are natural science and its application in industry and commerce through machinery and the use of non-human modes of energy. . . .

Science has brought with it a radically novel conception of physical nature and of our relation to it. This new conception stands as yet side by side with the conception of the world and man that is a heritage from the past, especially from that Christian tradition through which the typically European social imagination has been formed. The things of the physical world and the moral realm have fallen apart, while the Greek tradition and that of the medieval age held them in intimate union—although a union accomplished by different means in the two periods. The opposition that now exists between the spiritual and ideal elements of our historic heritage and the structure of physical nature that is disclosed by science, is the ultimate source of the dualisms formulated by philosophy since Descartes and Locke. These formulations in turn reflect a conflict that is everywhere active in modern civilization. From one point of view the problem of recovering an organic place for art in civilization is like the problem of reorganizing our heritage from the past and the insights of our present knowledge into a coherent and integrated imaginative union.

The problem is so acute and widely influential that any solution that can be proposed is an anticipation that can at best be realized only by the course of events. . . . It is true that physical science strips its objects of the qualities that give the objects and scenes of ordinary experience all their poignancy and preciousness, leaving the world, as far as the scientific rendering of it is concerned, without the traits that have always constituted its immediate value. But the world of ordinary experience in which art operates, remains just what it was.[1]

According to this passage, there is, on the one hand, stuff or material itself indifferent to us and our aspirations, disenchanted (in Weber's famous phrase), and with its motions having no natural ends or purposes. This is the "radically novel conception of physical nature" that Dewey has in mind. At the very least, and metaphysics and epistemology to one side, it has served us well in many respects to think of nature in this way. Once we so conceive of nature, and then further carry out the appropriate investigations of the lawlike but nonpurposive behaviors of mere material things, then we can, sometimes, manipulate those things in order to satisfy desires, needs, and interests that we experience ourselves as just having. The modern scientific understanding of material nature lays the cognitive groundwork for practices and systems of, for example, medicine, transportation, communication, and industrial production that it would be difficult and undesirable to abandon.

And there is, on the other hand, us, we with our purposes—purposes that seem, in light of the disenchantment of things, ineluctably subjective, inner matters of groundless preference alone. If we should happen to be able to make use of material things to satisfy our preferences, great—and likewise great if two or more people should happen to have overlapping preferences. Finally, just as a matter of political compromise to avoid violence that threatens to inhibit all preference satisfaction, it is very often best not to enforce preferences: let individuals with their preferences be who they are and let them trade with one another in free markets as they wish. For most of us, at least in the developed worlds, life without modern technologies and modern market systems of production and exchange would be both unthinkable and undesirable.

Yet, as Dewey suggests, this picture, however ineluctably built into our culture, of an inner, subjective mental life, with only subjective purposes, facing off against an outer, material, objective but meaningless nature is also not an entirely happy one. For one thing, this picture affords no basis for objective assessment of pursuits of subjective interest, that is, no basis for appeals to justice or fairness that might constrain rapacious or exploitative behavior. It may be that a free market works efficiently to maximize preference satisfaction among traders with relatively equal holdings and stocks of information but different preferences, and there is therefore good reason at least sometimes to think of free markets as fair. But if imbalances in holdings, power, or information grow too great, or military might intervenes, or free riding is possible, then this institutional arrangement is likely to prove unstable. Then the guns or lawsuits start. And what then? If there are only individuals who are competing with one another for the material resources to satisfy subjective desires, then it is likely in the end to be guns rather than lawsuits. Lawsuits and court verdicts may be construed as themselves covert forms of violence. Family life and citizenship are all too likely to decay into what Hegel calls "particularity by itself, given free rein in every direction to satisfy its needs, accidental caprices, and subjective desires, [so that it] destroys itself and its substantive concept in this process of gratification."[2] Anarchy, both social and personal, is loosed upon the world. Plato predicts explicitly that this will happen in a pluralist, subjective democracy that lacks any metaphysically founded conception of justice.[3] There seems no longer to be any metaphysical standard for checking on what we do, and without one we seem likely to do just about anything, including a lot of fighting. Underlying this fighting, there is at least the risk that no one will really believe in the worth of a way of life. My preferences may seem to me to be just given and not to be of any worth to me or to anyone else. Why should I care about anything, I may worry? Subjective anomie, or what is generally now called depression, threatens us, and it is more or less endemic in modern industrial societies. And yet it would, again, be both difficult and undesirable to give up the benefits of modern science and its culture in order to revert to a more closed, traditionalist, metaphysically or religiously circumscribed way of life.

How, then, might we best think of ourselves and our place in nature so that we might both accept the benefits of modern science and democratic culture and yet avoid or at least curb their harms? This question has been raised for us by thinkers as various as Kant, Hegel, Marx, Dewey, and John Paul II, albeit that they each have quite different answers in view.

One particularly interesting suggestion for thinking about this problem comes from the eminent literary critic Northrop Frye.[4] The suggestion arises out of a very broad sketch Frye offers of the history of Western thought and language. According to Frye, there are three successive historical stages of basic styles of thought and language. The first stage is the metaphorical-mythological stage, as people tell stories simultaneously about what we now call physical events and about the meanings of things. Science and religion, natural cosmology and creation theory, historical reporting and primeval storytelling are all not yet sharply distinguished from one another. One sees the dawn or the spring as the coming of a beneficent divine presence, or one sees a storm as the divine wrath of the sea itself, understood as both a physical something and a personality. Frye identifies this stage of thought and culture with pastoral and nomadic life generally and with roughly Homeric Greece and the early Hebrew tradition in particular.

The metaphorical-mythological stage is then superseded by a metonymic-intellectual stage. Allegory becomes a dominant form, as signs are taken to indicate a deeper order of reality in relation to which our ordinary experience is only a surface. Access to this reality is claimed by educated elites, who consequently lay further claim to the administration of daily life and general culture. Justifications for how things are to be done are propounded by these elites, on the basis of their expert knowledge of the deeper and fuller reality. According to Frye, one can see something of this stage of thought and language as early as the pre-Platonic Protagorean tradition in Greece. It figures in Plato's dialogues, and then in Christianity, which Nietzsche famously described as Platonism for the masses. In Christianity from at least the Augustinian period onward, the liturgies and sacraments are administered by expert priests, and the regulation of daily life is referred to the reality described in the Bible, read aright in Latin by an educated minority. Late-medieval Everyman plays participate in this form of language and thought, as the ordinary person's life is seen as an allegory of the sufferings and possibilities of resurrection that were disclosed by Jesus and that inform the lives of all of us.

In the early modern period, progressively from roughly 1550 or 1600 and into the present, this metonymic-intellectual system is succeeded by a demotic-scientific-manipulative system. Modern scientific knowledge is available to anyone who takes the trouble to educate himself. As Descartes once remarked, "There are many things to do in life, and [a good man] has to direct that life in such a manner that the greater part of it shall remain to him for the performance of good actions, which his own reason ought to teach him, even supposing that he were to receive his lessons from it alone."[5] The very idea that there are many things to do in life—including at least discoveries to be made and technological devices to ameliorate our material situation to be invented—as opposed to one central thing that is to be done, namely living according to the will of God, is itself revolutionary. The further idea that we can use our reason to figure out how to do the many things we might do is equally far-reaching. As these ideas are worked out in modern scientific culture, enormous benefits accrue, while at the same time our modern political and moral lives become pluralized and, potentially, evacuated of meaning, in being no longer referred to a larger reality that is either metaphorically or metonymically accessible.

Like Kant and Hegel and Dewey, Frye, while accepting the benefits of modern scientific and technological culture, worries about this. He worries in particular that there is nothing any longer to hold us together within the terms of a common project. Without the ability to discern either metaphorically or metonymically possibilities and necessities of personal and cultural development that are latent within a larger reality itself, chaos threatens. We may fall into "the subordination of everything creative to the expediencies and superstitions of authority . . . [or we may] fly apart into a chaos of mutually unintelligible elites, of which those nearest the center of society would soon take control. So atavistic a regression, in the present stage of technological development, might well wipe the human race off the planet."[6] This passage is perhaps somewhat purple and apocalyptic, but the problem is clear. What, if anything, can any longer bring us together under a shared sense of common, objective possibilities of life and value? The old dispensations are dead, and for good reason, but a life lived without any objective dispensations threatens to be bleak, chaotic, and violent, or perhaps nasty, brutish, and short. The constructed institutions of the democratic state and the free market may, once again, intervene to moderate the problem. Social order and open trading are by no means insignificant institutional goods. But what is to prevent free riding and the domination of state and market institutions by the powerful?

This sense of a need for a new dispensation is the central *point de départ* for romantic thought and writing and for the thought of Kant, as he seeks to found a critical and constructive philosophy that avoids both traditionalist but baseless dogmatism and skeptical nomadism in life and in thought. Frye's own response to this need, building on Blake and on Blake's reading of the Bible, is to suggest that we can and should learn from the great poets and from the Bible to uncover and reactivate the myth of all mythologies: the tentative availability of a reconciled, pastoral, resurrected life. The idea is that we can, as it were, bypass the metonymic-intellectual stage of thought and regain contact with the metaphorical-mythological stage that remains present as a dim, underlying stratum of our lives. This is, Frye suggests, exactly what great poets and the writers of the great sacred texts, preeminently the Bible, do. Donald Marshall has elegantly summarized this strategy of recovery as it was pursued by Wordsworth:

In Wordsworth the synthetic, creative, and sympathetic power of imagination, nourished on a popular tradition of ballad and romance with roots in the great poetry pre-dating the Enlightenment, asserted itself against an instrumentalist reason, which in poetry took the form of a masquerade in the form of conscious and merely willed classicism. Wordsworth found the true source of imagination: in nature and particularly in the poet's experience of nature during childhood, when he was most open to its varied and spirited influence. The language in which this recollected experience was transformed into the guide of later life and feeling derived from the ordinary language of men, particularly rural men, whose lives preserved the great rhythms of pastoral and agricultural life, recorded in and mediated by the Bible, anonymous folk poetry, and related literary forms.[7]

In *The Romantic Legacy*, Charles Larmore has similarly argued that the romantic imagination functions to express and recover senses of community and of belonging to place, though he aptly notes also a contending sense of romantic irony, as the poet simultaneously feels apart from others in the possession of distinctive education and creative power.[8]

This romantic sense of a recovery through imagination of a suppressed stratum of thought, language, and experience, so that we might once again feel ourselves to have a common situation and objective purposiveness, is a wonderful idea. But, as the careers and receptions of Blake and Wordsworth show, it will not be so easy to carry it out in a way that significantly influences public life. Those who pursue this strategy are all too likely to be dismissed as dreamers or balkanized as objects of mostly private, merely religioaesthetic reverence and reverie, at least in relation to serious questions of social policy that require fully worked out schemes for institutions. Can imagination, poetry, myth, and metaphor make high cognitive claims on us? On many or most of us? And what institutions will then serve? As Hegel noted in criticizing romanticism,[9] a sense of subjective inwardness informs a good deal of romantic writing, as poets despite their best intentions for social effect withdraw into rehearsals of the progress of their own imaginations, as in Wordsworth ever withdrawing from work on *The Recluse* to write *The Prelude* instead. The thought that romantics withdraw from the world in order to find solace in nature has informed much of the reception of romanticism, in the sense in which Jerome McGann has criticized romantic*ism*—that is, the dominant teaching of romantic poetry within departments of literature up until, say, 1980—for its subjectively cultic character. (McGann distinguishes between institutionalized romanticism and a tougher, stranger, more self-critical romantic writing.)[10] When one then further takes into account a sense, inherited from Freud, of the anarchistic pressures placed by our sexual lives on both individual development and imaginative production, then the prospects for cultural restoration via romantic imagining grow even bleaker. And then there are the categories that are reinforced every day by an increasingly global commodity culture: subjective preference, taste, and want, which stand against objective production costs and processes. How is imaginative art to make a public claim on us in the midst of the domination of social life by these categories of thought and experience?

The address to our cultural situation that is offered us by romantic imagining has considerable pertinence and power. Given, however, the evident difficulties that attach to carrying out a romantic renovation of culture, it is worthwhile considering what other possibilities of general address to our cultural circumstances are on the books. Three further stances, each significantly different from romanticism, can be usefully distinguished.

The first is "Relaxed Naturalism" or "Just Coping" or, to give it a proper name, Humeanism, alluding to Hume's remark that we should acknowledge "the whimsical condition of mankind, who must act and reason and believe; though they are not able, by their most diligent enquiry, to satisfy themselves concerning the foundation of these operations, or to remove the objections, which may be raised against them."[11] One might, that is, think that there are properly or realistically no such things as an objective plight or an objective destiny to be recovered. There are, rather, just many people who want many different things, in a situation in which material resources for satisfying wants are simply moderately scarce but not altogether lacking. This is perhaps generally the situation in the North Atlantic democracies. Richard Rorty had the habit of claiming that these democracies offer us, as a merely contingent possibility that we have somehow invented or stumbled upon, a comparatively good enough way of life. Talk of achieving our destiny is to be rejected as pretty much amounting to the nostalgia of the priests. This Rortian view has considerable currency, at least for public life, against the more religious visions of Alasdair MacIntyre and Charles Taylor. Assignments and enforcements of human rights can be defended as matters of pragmatic compromise, given the practical necessities of at least some social cooperation. In

Quine's elegant phrase, morality becomes a matter of "birch rod and sugar plum."[12] That is, there are certain behaviors that we more or less decide to reward and to punish, because rewarding and punishing these behaviors works well enough to keep us going and to enable us to satisfy some of our wants. We can drop all talk of renovation, destiny, and objective purpose. In political life, elbow room or negative liberty is good enough. Privately, a bit of Millian experimentalism in lifestyles is not really a bad thing. This is, perhaps, the dominant view of life in northern Europe and the "Blue States" of the United States nowadays. It is unlikely that it will pass away any time soon, and it is not at all clear that its passing would be desirable. It offers us a fair amount of independence from authoritarian comprehensive enforcements of social visions. This view urges us and even enables us one by one, or affinity group by affinity group, or as citizens who share at least some bits of history, just to do the best we can. There is at least a hint of this view in even John Dewey, alongside the strains of moral and cultural perfectionism in his work.

The difficulty of this view, already suggested, is that it leaves public life open to manipulation by powerful elites. It encourages free riding and an insidiously creeping social chaos and decline, as Plato and MacIntyre have argued. It makes it difficult to believe in one's way of life, so that social anomie and depression threaten. It has trouble figuring out what to do in real crisis situations, where there are not many relevant experiences and not many rules of thumb on which to draw.

The second view is Cartesianism. The cognitive and technological benefits of the Cartesian conception of disenchanted, material nature are manifest. But in addition to these cognitive and technological benefits, there is also an attractive moral, spiritual stance associated with this conception of nature and with the relation of mind to it. As Charles Taylor notes, Descartes furthers an

ethic of rational control that find[s] its sources in a sense of dignity and self-esteem [by] transpos[ing] *inward* something of the spirit of the honour ethic. . . . Strength, firmness, resolution, control, these are the crucial qualities, a subset of the warrior-aristocratic virtues, but now internalized. They are not deployed in great deeds of military valor in public space, but rather in the inner domination of passion by thought. . . . Descartes constantly enjoins efficacious action for what we want [so that we may become "masters and possessors of nature"], alongside detachment from the outcome.[13]

As Descartes puts it in the *Discourse*,

My third maxim was always to try especially to conquer myself rather than fortune, to change my desires rather than the order of the world; and generally to become accustomed to believing that there is nothing that is utterly within our power, except for our thoughts, so that, after having done our best regarding things external to us, everything that fails to bring us success, from our point of view, is absolutely impossible.[14]

But satisfaction in correct thinking is virtually infinite. Thus Descartes argues that if we learn to follow correctly the proper principles for scientific investigation, then we can comport ourselves both with pride in our cognitive achievements and with humility, in acknowledgment of the limits of our finite understanding. Pride where knowledge and, sometimes, consequent technology are achievable, coupled with stoicism about our limits, leading to ataraxia or blessedness, is an available stance that has genuine charms. Descartes himself writes that we may, if we take up this stance, "rival the gods in their happiness" and experience "intense satisfaction" than which there is nothing "sweeter or more innocent . . . in this life."[15]

It would be folly to underestimate either the practical-technological or the moral-spiritual benefits of this stance. But it too faces problems. This stance does not point to any practices or styles of expressive action in politics, family life, or interpersonal relations generally. It is expressed directly only in cognitive practice, leaving everything else either to be ignored, to be coped with as a matter of convenience, or to be sorted out via the practical, ultimately market-structured adjustment of preferences. There is no distinctive worth or dignity attaching to any particular mode of interpersonal, familial, social, or political life. Thus Descartes remarks that, apart from the practice of natural science, "the most useful course of action was to rule myself in accordance with those with whom I had to live,"[16] whether Persians, Chinese, or Frenchman. This policy kept Descartes free from the Inquisition, and it supports considerable broad-minded tolerance of what are ultimately the follies of one or another human group in interpersonal matters, where no well-founded rules are available. But it does not support the achievement of intimacy. It is hard to see how Descartes could tell the difference between getting along with a wife and getting along with the Chinese. It is, therefore, no accident that he never married, and the philosophical problem of other minds that arises in his work is itself perhaps a reflection of a pervasive sense of alienation from other human beings.

The third stance is Byronism. Byron's own literary and theoretical writings are less interesting systematically than those of any of Blakean-Wordsworthian romanticism, Humeanism, or Cartesianism. But there can nonetheless be little doubt that Byron both summed up and stands for a certain cultural stance, the stance that Bertrand Russell called Byronism as "Titanic cosmic self-assertion,"[17] especially in matters sexual. Byron's own (let us call it) passionate and exuberant personal life expresses this stance, at least in part. And there has always been a well-motivated temptation to identify Byron with certain of his characters. Childe Harold, for example, is introduced to us as follows, in terms that seem to apply as well to Byron himself.

> Whileome in Albion's isle there dwelt a youth,
> Who ne in virtue's ways did take delight;
> But spend his days in riot most uncouth,
> And vexed with mirth the drowsy ear of Night.
> Ah, me! in sooth he was a shameless wight,
> Sore given to revel and ungodly glee;
> Few earthly things found favor in his sight

Save concubines and carnal companie,
And flaunting wassailers of high and low degree.[18]

Four stanzas later, we learn that he is not much given to repentance.

For he through Sin's long labyrinth had run,
Nor made atonement when he did amiss.[19]

The reasons for taking up a stance of passionate self-assertion, if reasons are in view, is that it is better to feel something, and in particular to feel one's own powers of command, than to feel nothing at all, albeit that the rate or variety or artistic imaginativeness of conquest may have to be increased in order to get the same effect in feeling, addiction being what it is. This is the stance that we can also see in Don Giovanni and in the seducer Johannes of Kierkegaard's *Either/Or*. This is largely the popular conception of romanticism. As one fairly simple commentary for students puts it, "In essence, Romanticism was, for a time, the triumph of feeling over thinking, the head over the heart."[20] Romanticism so construed or, better, Byronism, does help to remind us of the felt character of our own inner lives. We can, and often do, feel intensely, without much prior reasoning or policy formation but nonetheless with a kind of imaginative involvement, blending anticipation, recollection, and fantasy, in a manner not present in the lives of other creatures. The power thus to feel with imaginative involvement is one, it seems, that we wish not to repudiate, even if we could. We give it free rein in adolescence, perhaps, or on Halloween, or for Carnival, or for Las Vegas weekends. The liability, of course, is that it is hard to see how to build a stable life out of the cultivation of the pursuit of this kind of intensity of feeling, as Faust is brought in the end to realize.

So we have these three stances—Humeanism, Cartesianism, and Byronism, against which I have posed a more genuine romanticism, associated with Blake and Wordsworth. All three of these stances are lived—Cartesianism for science and planning, Humeanism for buying and selling and for semistable social relations, Byronism for holidays. When they are thus lived together, in uneasy pragmatic compromise with each other, then what we have is the pragmatic liberalism that Gary Gutting has eloquently defended.[21] This pragmatic compromise solution has a good claim to being our form of life, at least in the more or less well-off North Atlantic democracies and in the Blue States: naturalist rejection of comprehensive religious enforcements, Cartesianism for science, and Byronism on the side, all adopted because they seem to be what works best, pragmatically, in their particular spheres.

The question, then, is how stable this pragmatic compromise is. Or does it rather suffer from the liabilities of each stance taken individually, plus the added problem that each stance places pressure on the others? For example, Cartesianism may point toward the management of culture by so-called technical experts, rather than compromise, thus undermining democracy. Or Humeanism may undermine commitment to science as a vocation. Or Byronism may threaten to undermine just about anything. Just who are we, and where are we going?

In this situation, we might conjecture that the Wordsworthian romanticism first sketched offers us something of a middle way, since it accepts elements of Cartesianism, Humeanism, and Byronism but, unlike pragmatism, thinks of maintaining this acceptance as a continuing task. The characteristic Wordsworthian romantic writer—Wordsworth—unlike the Byronic romantic writer, is a continual scrutinizer of the terms of our current mixed settlement. Wordsworth is worried about the rise of a modern scientific culture in which a sense of value and meaning is lost. But, like Hume, he is unwilling, at least in his major writings, to accept comprehensive political enforcements of religious stances. He is too much of an individualist for that. He has a Byronic sense of the power and importance of his own imagination and his imaginative responses to events, but he seeks also to keep his imagination apt to the persons and events he encounters, where the marker of accuracy is that others can be brought to share in his imaginative responses, thus confirming them. Thus his poetic imagination courts not only excess and poetic glory but also depth of common response to common predicaments and possibilities of life. In the *Prelude*, he undertakes to "speak / A lasting inspiration,"[22] as he retraces his own fostering "alike by beauty and by fear."[23] The point of this rehearsal is not simply the particularities of his own life but further that within these particularities one can "trace / Our Being's earthly progress,"[24] thus showing, as it were, the universal, or what is possible and valuable for us all, in the particular, that is, in the details of growing up in the Lake District, studying (or mostly partying) at Cambridge, traveling in France, and so on. The moral of this rehearsal is that "these objects"—that is, the beautiful and the sublime—should "everlastingly affect the mind."[25] The experience of the sublime awakens in us a felt sense of our own rational and expressive powers and dignity, so that we do not settle for Humean coping or trying to get what we already take ourselves to want, but instead seek to deploy and express our human powers originally. The experience of the beautiful connects us to the common, so that both Byronic excessiveness and Cartesian alienation are avoided. Throughout these rehearsals, Wordsworth continually questions his own progress in writing and avoids conclusive dogmatism. He wonders whether his tracing of his progress is really as exemplary as he hopes and whether his audience will receive him or repudiate him—indeed, whether his audience exists at all. Since the poet has "the task of *creating* the taste by which he is to be enjoyed,"[26] it may not. In rehearsing his own history, Wordsworth has trouble finding the plot and its moral. We have in the *Prelude*, he writes to Coleridge, "Turned and returned with intricate delay."[27] Yet the very ongoing effort to find the plot and to establish the importance of the experiences of both the sublime and the beautiful is itself the self-modifying way to balance Humeanism, Cartesianism, and Byronism against one another. This Wordsworthian practice of seeking expressive power in connection with the common is always crossed with self-questioning rather than dominated by a preformulated plan or conclusion. Engaging in this practice is what the best artists and literary writers, in particular situations, do.

One consequence of this conception of the seriousness of Wordsworthian romanticism is that there is no great romantic drama. The reason for this is that Wordsworthian romanticism lingers in the activity of accepting and working through conflicting commitments, as it accepts the attractiveness within consciousness of all of Humeanism, Cartesianism, and Byronism. It seeks to bring these stances into fuller and more coherent communication with one another within consciousness, so that more human, more expressive action can be achieved. It is no accident that Harold Bloom once described romantic poetry as the internalization of quest romance.[28] The action of romantic drama is internal to consciousness itself. But this internalization of action then cuts against the possibility of presenting important dramatic conflicts between different characters, if these characters are themselves to be complex enough to participate in the movement of romantic consciousness. The only real candidates for great romantic dramas are Goethe's *Faust* and Shakespeare's tragedies and comedies, so far as one finds confrontation between emergent, modern individualism and valuable, stable commitments to be central to them. But these dramas work so magnificently precisely because the claims on the individual of an existing external culture of honor, religion, nation, or clan as they stand are taken seriously against modern individualism, even if individualism turns out to be an irrepudiable force. Once its irrepudiability is fully accepted, then the drama is internalized, as individuals must sort out ever anew their standing conflicting commitments. (Hamlet is poised on the edge of accepting this irrepudiability, without yet being crassly individualistic.) Modern and modernist lyric and the modern novel can survive and flourish because they are able to focus on the interior life of protagonists in a way that modern drama, with its rejection of the artificiality of the extended soliloquy, cannot. The drama of modern life is largely that of individuals coming to terms—or, increasingly, bleakly failing to come to terms, as in Beckett—within their own consciousness or within restricted spheres of conversation, with how they are to stand in relation to the conflicting attractive possibilities afforded by, or latent within, a culture.

But what if one were to undertake to write a drama about the fact that modern life offers no ready way to blend naturalness (either Byronic-spontaneous or Humean-customary) with originality (either Cartesian-intellectual or Byronic-spontaneous)? (Beckett rejects ready blending, but by reducing his characters to the barely discursively percipient and his cultures to completely desiccated routines. He thus undervalues complexity, energy, and adaptive responsiveness in both individuals and cultures.) Could one *show* Byronic types, Cartesian types, and Humean types somehow in interaction with one another, as types, while also intimating that these types represent aspects of us all, in our own divided commitments? What work could such a showing do? Could it point toward any kind of fuller acknowledgment of our complexities?

These are the questions that Tom Stoppard takes up in *Arcadia*. Stoppard accepts the structural necessity for drama of presenting conflict between characters, and he also rejects the extended Shakespearean soliloquy. We see his characters doing what they do, but we do not hear or overhear them in their internal movements of mind as they are pulled now toward Humeanism, now toward Cartesianism, now toward Byronism. Stoppard also refuses the great marriage plot, as in Jane Austen, within which plot two characters work out the possibility of a good enough life together, as they find their commitments and talents complemented in each other.

The action in *Arcadia* takes place, instead, in a kind of public space that we witness from a privileged standpoint, able to watch without being ourselves watched. Stoppard's method of dramatic construction is juxtaposition. The characters are largely types, with Thomasina as a Cartesian figure (with a bit of Byronism struggling to get out); Septimus as a Byronic figure (overlaid with the surface Cartesianism of a Cambridge education); Hannah as a cooler mixture of Cartesian scholarship with modern Humean, tolerant whimsy at the follies of mankind; and Valentine as a contemporary Cartesian. Other characters are even closer to pure types in a way that makes for farce, as they are dominated by particular varieties of ambition and vanity. They think of themselves as something they are not: Bernard takes himself to be a scholar; Ezra takes himself to be a poet. The remaining characters are largely incidental to the action taking place between the principal, more rounded four (Thomasina, Septimus, Hannah, and Valentine) and the two figures of farce (Ezra and Bernard). Stoppard sets his characters as types within a space that we can witness, and he waits to see what happens. To some extent, his method of juxtaposition deliberately shirks the internal development of character and the working through of conflicting commitments in favor of the charms of farce.

Stoppard himself is quite aware of how his dramatic method of the juxtaposition of types works. As he remarked in an interview, "I don't think *Arcadia* says very much about these two sides of the human personality or temperament [that is, the Cartesian and the Byronic]. . . . And yet it's firing all around the target, making a pattern around the target."[29] He reports that his favorite line in modern English drama is "I'm a man of no convictions—at least I *think* I am," from Christopher Hampton's *The Philanthropist*.[30] He observes that he "writes plays because writing dialogue is the only respectable way of contradicting yourself."[31] He describes his objective as "to perform a marriage between a play of ideas and a farce. . . . [This objective] represents two sides of my own personality, which can be described as seriousness compromised by my frivolity, or . . . frivolity redeemed by my seriousness."[32] "Happiness is equilibrium. Shift your weight,"[33] he remarks in his own voice, quoting his character Henry from *The Real Thing*. What all these remarks indicate is a shying—perhaps as a result of the necessities of dramatic presentation, perhaps from overwhelming shyness expressed as wit, perhaps because of the sheer complexities of modern life—from working through, from thinking. Juxtaposition, pattern, contradiction, equilibrium—these trump internalization and the working through of thoughts, ideas, attitudes, and emotions.

And yet, as J. L. Austin once wrote, "there's the bit where you say it and the bit where you take it back."[34] When *Arcadia* opened in 1993 in London and in 1995 in New York, it was widely (though not without exception)[35] praised as a breakthrough in character development and emotional expressiveness and as a move, in particular, beyond the consistently arch and dryly intellectual quality of his earlier work.[36]

As Tim Appelo put the point in his review in *The Nation*, "Unlike the spy-jive mac-guffins he juggles in *Hapgood*, the mystery addressed in *Arcadia* is one to which Stoppard is fully emotionally committed."[37] There is something to this point, and it has mostly to do with the concluding scene, where the two worlds—those of 1809 and of the present—as it were overlap. Here is where, at last, we see not farce and wordplay and juxtaposition but development in character, consciousness, and relationship. First Thomasina and Septimus, and then Hannah and Gus, waltz. These parallel waltzes have the feel of a dream. They are surprising—especially so in that, like dreams, they contravene time in occurring together. This gives them the feel of being somehow mythical or eternally recurring, something that ever haunts us. The waltzing together of these pairs, across time, has the fuguelike feeling of something half occurrent and half remembered.

The absence of dialogue during this waltzing is prepared by Valentine's earlier remark that he's given up on his analysis of the rise and fall of the grouse population on the Coverly estate because there's "Too much noise. There's just too much bloody noise."[38] (Too many unpredictable external factors induce deviations in the population that prevent any natural pattern from being evident.) This remark alerts us that we may, at least sometimes, find sense in silence rather than in speech. In this final waltzing, and in the overlapping of the two time periods, we find "patterns making themselves out of nothing."[39] We are left with a sense that the problems of human subjects struggling to express their emotional and intellectual subjectivities fully, originally, and with each other within settings of thermodynamically decaying nature and stale culture persist, making us above all interesting animals. But despite their persistence, a significant response to these problems may be, for a time, possible. Thomasina remarks to Septimus, "there is another geometry which I am engaged in discovering by trial and error."[40] Stoppard's juxtapositions work similarly, allowing a geometry or a set of shapes of human life, intelligence, and desire to show themselves.

The dreamlike, fuguelike feeling of the final waltzing is further reinforced by the fact that it is these pairs of characters who waltz, in particular by the fact that these waltzes are for each of them a kind of breakthrough. Septimus acknowledges Thomasina's just-about-adult sexuality, which has now come to expression along with her intelligence. In doing so, he further acknowledges his own depth of attraction to her as a person, to her embodied intelligence, thus overcoming his earlier libertinism in favor of something more like love. Hannah acknowledges Gus's pain and neediness and intelligence in his silence, thus lending depth of responsiveness to her own typical professional scholarly scrupulousness. Although she has earlier stuck to detachment, insisting to Chloe that "I don't want a dancing partner, least of all Mr. Nightingale. I don't dance,"[41] she too is now able to dance, a bit awkwardly, when the right partner comes along at the right time. In inviting her to dance, Gus acknowledges her intelligence and passion together, in taking her as fit for dancing, thus acknowledging, too, that words and feelings can coexist in a single character: depth of feeling need not always engender muteness, and cleverness need not always suppress feeling. It is as though the two parts of the soul—analytical intelligence and depth of feeling, Cartesianism and Byronism—have at last been put together, at least for a moment, according to the logic of a dream, across time, and surrounded by music rather than parsed out in words. Is this final scene, blending disjoint times and moving to music, without words, an escape from actuality into form or a registering of human need and possibility? It is inescapable to ask this question, but it is not clear that it is necessary to answer it one way or the other.

According to this scene and the logic that prepares it, the Wordsworthian practice of bringing the parts of the soul together, in pursuit of expressive fluency in thought and feeling and action, in relation to others and to what is common, both informs and haunts human life. But the work of this practice remains always in part unfinished. As Hannah remarks, "It's wanting to know that makes us matter. . . . Better to struggle on knowing that failure is final."[42] We will remain interesting animals, in pursuit of fullness of fluency and at-homeness as subjects that we will never quite achieve. The dancing of these pairs—their real physical movement and intimacy, yet somehow outside historical time and "for us" as observing audience—offers a clarifying catharsis of what is possible for us. But, in Marcuse's words, "the reconciliation which the catharsis offers also preserves the irreconcileable."[43] The space of dramatic art is not joined to the space we occupy as viewers and then as agents. The marking of this magical, dramatic space where some provisional reconciliation takes place as outside of time and as other to us testifies to what Adorno called our continuing "suffering in an existence alien to the subject"; the dancing that these pairs are able to achieve as human agents testifies "to love for it as well."[44] We both recognize ourselves in these characters and remain aware of their occupying a space of art that we can, would, and yet cannot occupy wholly in daily life. *Arcadia* itself closes with this dancing and so is silent—bleakly, pregnantly, undecidably—about the rest of life.

Serious writing must find some way to show that moments, perhaps even ones of considerable scope and duration, of good enough fluency and at-homeness are possible, if it is not to reduce us to ignorant and empty sites of mere coping with life. Yet it must also accept that such moments do not last forever, especially in light of modern complexities of desire and social life, and that there is no formula for either achieving or sustaining them. It must accept a constitutive incompleteness—accept, that is, its own failure to track the achievement of any final happiness, if it is to be faithful to the lack of final happiness in human life. It must somehow avoid denying human finitude and temporality in complacent dogmatism while also succeeding in showing sometime achievements of expressive, embodied intelligence and the satisfaction of desire, as in dancing. This astonishing concluding scene in *Arcadia* manages to blend skepticism and acknowledgment of finitude with the presentation of apt, fluent feeling and of gratitude for life. "In the silence you don't know, you must go on, I can't go on, I'll go on."[45]

3.

Romantic Subjectivity in Goethe and Wittgenstein

As a result of the fine work of Mark Rowe, Joachim Schulte, and Gordon Baker and Peter Hacker,[1] it has now been evident for some time that there are deep affinities—affinities in style and textual organization, in conceptions of elucidatory explanation via comparisons, and in a sense of subjectivity housed within nature—between the Goethe of the *Farbenlehre* and the Wittgenstein of *Philosophical Investigations*. Among the very deepest of these affinities is their shared sense of the limits of metaphysical explanation. The identification of simple elements is always relative to purposes and circumstances, never ultimate. Hence there is no single kind of ultimate explanation running from the nature and behavior of ultimate simples to the nature and behavior of complexes composed out of them. There are often useful explanations to be found of how the behaviors of complexes are determined by the behaviors of their parts, but this kind of explanation is one among many. Comparative descriptions of complexes—whether of organisms, human practices, works of art, or chemical and physical structures—are not to be supplanted in favor of ultimate metaphysical explanation.

Valuable and sound though these ideas are, they are, however, not the theme here. Instead, a different form of affinity between Goethe and Wittgenstein is more in view—a substantive affinity in their senses of what it is to be a human subject. Methodological and general metaphysical affinities are taken for granted; beyond or behind them lie affinities of substance in their conceptions of human life. Thomas Mann's remarks on *Die Leiden des jungen Werthers* provide a useful starting point. "It would," Mann observes,

not be a simple task to analyze the psychic state that determined the underpinning of European civilization at that time [1774, the date of publication of *Werther*]. . . . A discontent with civilization, an emancipation of emotions, a gnawing yearning for a return to the natural and elemental, a shaking at the shackles of ossified culture, a revolt against convention and bourgeois confinement: everything converged to create a spirit that came up against the limitations of individuation itself, that allowed an effusive, boundless affirmation of life to take on the form of a death wish. Melancholy and discontent with the rhythmical monotony of life was the norm.[2]

It is likewise not a simple task to say what may have made such melancholy and discontent the norm, at least in certain circles. Secularization, bringing with it a sense of lost meaningfulness as religious ritual became a smaller part of daily life, and modernization, bringing with it a market economy and new but very uncertain life chances, are surely part of the story. But secularization and modernization are themselves interwoven with deep, largely tacit self-understandings about what is worth doing, in ways that are difficult to disentangle. Charles Taylor, in his monumental survey of the making of the modern identity, describes what he calls "three major facets of this identity: first, modern inwardness, the sense of ourselves as beings with inner depths; second, the affirmation of ordinary life which develops from the early modern period; third, the expressivist notion of nature as an inner moral source."[3] These facets of identity that come to the fore in modernity are as much a part of a widely available human repertoire of identity as they are byproducts of something else. They are, according to Taylor, an inescapable part of our moral framework, a set of commitments that we cannot help but have, even where they also sit uneasily against one another, as the claims of the ordinary pull against the pursuit of original expressive power.

One important result of these commitments is an undecomposable intermingling of moral discovery with moral invention. We no longer think of ourselves as simply living out in one way or another basic human tendencies that are simply given. Rather, drawing on our reflective inwardness, on ordinary life, and on natural energies, we partly make ourselves what we are. As Taylor puts it, "We find the sense of life through articulating it. And moderns have become acutely aware of how much sense being there for us depends on our own powers of expression. Discovering here depends on, is interwoven with, inventing."[4] Finding is inseparable from founding.

But why should this occasion what Mann noted: discontent, yearning, shaking, revolt, melancholy, and a death wish? It is easy enough to see why a certain improvisatoriness and independence of mind might be valued. But how and why did our moral improvisations come to be freighted with all that? Here the answer has to do with a certain lack of both ground and closure to our moral efforts. Without fixed tendencies and *tele* as starting points and endpoints, it becomes uncertain what moral progress and human achievement might look like—even uncertain whether they are possible at all. Philippe Lacoue-Labarthe and Jean-Luc Nancy note the uncertainties that attach to our moral efforts in the wake of the felt absence of any fixed presentation of the self and its powers, as they describe the conception of the subject in Kant's moral theory.

> Without oversimplifying or hardening the contours of a question that merits extended analysis, we cannot fail to note that this "subject" of morality can be defined only negatively, as a subject that is not the subject of knowledge (this knowledge suppressed "to make room for belief"), as a subject without *mathesis*, even

of itself. It is indeed posited as freedom, and freedom is the locus of "self-consciousness." But this does not imply that there
is any cognition—or even consciousness—of freedom. . . . [T]he
question of [the moral subject's] unity, and thus of its very "being subject," is brought to a pitch of high tension.[5]

Lacking a fixed ground and definite *telos*, efforts at articulating
and enacting "a sense of life" come to be marked by a desperate intensity. Different subjects become variously lost within different ongoing projects of articulation, each maintaining its sense of its place
and progress not through ratification by an audience, which is all too
caught up in its own projects, but rather through a hysterical lingering in process. Articulation "sets out to penetrate the essence of poiesy
[poetic making], in which the [articulation] produces the truth of
production itself . . . the truth of production *of itself*, of autopoiesy."[6]
The manifold modern *Bildungsromanen* and personal epics of coming to self-consciousness and assured social vocation, but specifically
Bildungsromanen and epics that have difficulty in reaching their own
conclusions (other, perhaps, than by taking the artistic making of the
very work in hand as the achieved *telos*), are evidence of the domi-
nance of the project of autopoiesis in the modern moral imagination.
Human moral self-imagination and achievement become a "question
of the *becoming* present of the highest,"[7] not of its *being* present.

The three inescapable parts of our moral framework that Taylor
identifies—inwardness, ordinary life, and nature as an expressive re-
source—conspire in our experience with and against one another to
inhibit the achievement of a stable sense of life. Either nature in the
aspect of the sublime conspires with inwardness to resist the sways
of ordinary life and conventionality, thus setting up the image of the
chthonic genius as the exemplar of moral achievement, as in Nietzsche,
or nature in the aspect of the beautiful conspires with ordinary life
and conventionality, thus setting up an image of pastoralized domesticity as the exemplar of moral achievement, as in certain moments
in Rousseau. Each image then stands in immediate criticism of the
other, and no stable image of moral achievement persists.

Under such uncertainties and instabilities, it is all too plausible that one might not only become melancholic but come to wish for nothing more than surcease, even to regard the taking of one's own life as the only possible creative act with a fixed endpoint, as the only meaningful act. Or of course, more modestly, one might forego efforts to live according to a sense of life or to what is highest and assume instead an instrumentalist stance toward the things of life, seeking only modest satisfactions. This strategy is common in modernity, and it is surely honorable. But does it quite escape the silent melancholies, quiet desperations, and covert nihilisms about which Emerson and Thoreau and Nietzsche variously warned us?

To come now specifically to *Werther*: Werther's own character is torn between the idealized images of chthonic originality, represented for him by the wild excesses of his own inner emotional life, and pastoralized domesticity, represented for him by the figure of Lotte, maternally feeding bread to her younger brothers and sisters. There are interesting historical specificities that surround the split in Werther's character—and in Goethe's—between these two ideals. In his monumental study of Goethe's development, Nicholas Boyle suggests that these ideals are posed, and posed as irresolvable, for Werther and for Goethe, by certain strains in eighteenth-century German culture. "Werther's innermost life," he writes,

> is determined by a public mood; he lives out to the last, and inflicts on those around him, the loyalties which—because they are literary, intellectual, in a sense imaginary loyalties, generated within the current media of communication—most of his contemporaries take only half-seriously. His obsessions are not gratuitously idiosyncratic—they belong to his real and socially determined character, not just to a pathologically self-absorbed consciousness.[8]

Specifically, Boyle suggests that Leibnizianism, pietism, and sentimentalism offered images to Goethe of "the self thirsting for its perfectly adequate object."[9] This thirsting of the self for a confirming object took an especially inwardized turn in Germany, since it could not plausibly be welded to a project of political nation building. Autonomy or achieved selfhood had to be found within, and its principal marks were inner intensities of imagination, feeling, and devotion. Goethe's subjectivity, like Werther's, is dominated by "his belief in binding moments of insight"[10] to be achieved fitfully against the sway of official and conventional culture. At the same time, however, Goethe also absorbed a certain political realism and social consciousness from the Storm and Stress movement. He had an awareness of individual character types, including his own, as specific social roles—a novelist's sense (unlike anything in Werther himself) of social reality as narratable from multiple points of view. In *Werther*, as Boyle characterizes it, "the Sentimentalist content of the novel is in perfect but momentary balance with a Storm and Stress aesthetic which determines the manner of its presentation."[11] Like Werther, Goethe in writing *Werther* "endeavored to find roles for himself to act out which both had some general moral or historical significance and could be filled by him with a sense of selfhood: roles which fused both a [social] character and [an intensely individual] consciousness."[12] Inwardness and the pursuit of chthonic originality alone lead to empty solipsism; acceptance of oneself as a social type and conformity to convention alone lead to derivativeness and imaginative death. The task is to combine the pursuit of originality with acceptance of oneself as a social type. Unlike Werther, Goethe himself carried out this task through the act of writing about his innermost emotions and self-imaginations in a social setting. This act of writing gave him the opportunity both to cultivate his inner life and to achieve a certain realistic distance from it. For Werther, faced with the same task and torn between his hyperbolic idealizations of originality on the one hand and domesticity on the other, things do not go so well. The "very impetus to self-destruction is being imposed on him by the German public mind"—itself faced with the problem of cultivating both autonomous selfhood and continuing sociality—"commerce with which he cannot avoid, or wish to avoid, if he is to express himself at all."[13] The task of blending selfhood with social identity is unique neither to Werther, nor to Goethe, nor to the German public mind of the late eighteenth century. It is the fate of modern subjectivity as such either to face or to evade it. A sense of this problem as pressing and not to be evaded then arises with special intensity in late eighteenth-century Germany, in the wake of sentimentalism (itself a response to modernization and secularization) and in a hyperfractured political actuality.

Like Boyle, Mann too characterizes Werther as "the overrefined final product of the Christian-Pietist cult of the soul and of the emotions."[14] What this means, above all, is a desire for singularity, specifically a desire to desire, intensely and infinitely. As Mann puts it, "the desire to exchange that which is confining and conditional for that which is infinite and limitless is the fundamental character of Werther's nature, as it is of Faust's. . . . He is in love even before his love has an object."[15] Even Lotte asks Werther, "Why must you love me, me only, who belongs to another? I fear, I fear, that it is only the impossibility of possessing me that makes your desire for me so strong."[16] Only a desire for the impossible can certify itself as genuinely singular and original, capable of confirming selfhood against the grain of conventionality.

In the grip of such a desire, impossibly seeking original selfhood both against the grain of all conventionality and yet blended with social identity, no one knows what to do. Our desires are original if and only if impossible, unrecognizable—and they are recognizable and satisfiable if and only if they are mimes of the conventionalized desires of others. No wonder Werther observes that "all learned teachers and tutors agree that children do not understand the cause of their desires; but no one likes to think that adults too wander about this earth like children, not knowing where they come from or where they are going, not acting in accord with genuine motives, but ruled like children by biscuits, sugarplums, and the rod—and yet it seems to me so obvious" (9). Werther cannot anywhere recognize, act on, and satisfy his own desire as his own.

As he then himself wanders the earth, impossibly seeking fully original selfhood blended with social identity, Werther alternates in his moments of attachment and identification between surrender to beautiful scenes of sociality, composure, convention, and pastoralized domesticity, on the one hand, and ecstatic abandonment to sublime scenes of wild creative energy, on the other. In neither moment is the attachment or abandonment either ordinary or in fact achieved; in both cases it is hyperbolized in Werther's imagination into something exceptional, and his hyperbolizing imagination blocks his actually doing anything.

The emblem in nature of the beautiful, of pastoralized domesticity, and of attachment, in Werther's imaginative perception, is the cozy valley of Wahlheim—home's choice. "It is," Werther writes early on,

> interestingly situated on a hill, and by following one of the footpaths out of the village, you can have a view of the whole valley below you. A kindly woman keeps a small inn there, selling wine, beer, and coffee; and she is extremely cheerful and pleasant in spite of her age. The chief charm of this spot consists in two linden trees, spreading their enormous branches over the little green before the church, which is entirely surrounded by peasants' cottages, barns, and homesteads. Seldom have I seen a place so intimate and comfortable. (10)

The force and direction of Werther's idealization is evident in his litany of adjectives: "kindly," "small," "cheerful," "pleasant," "little," "intimate," and "comfortable." Here he would—originally and creatively—surrender himself to a domesticated, given, human life in nature. But to desire to do this originally and creatively is to make one unable to do it, and Werther simply gazes on the scene until, as he thinks of himself, he reverts in thought to the idea of nature as also a source of iconoclastic creative energy.

The counterpart scene in which Werther imagines ecstatically abandoning himself to the sublime comes late in his correspondence, as things are not going well. On December 12, he writes:

> Sometimes I am oppressed, not by apprehension or fear, but by an inexpressible inner fury which seems to tear up my heart and choke me. It's awful, awful. And then I wander about amid the horrors of the night, at this dreadful time of the year.

Yesterday evening it drove me outside. A rapid thaw had suddenly set in: I had been told that the river had risen, that the brooks had all overflowed their banks, and that the whole valley of Wahlheim was under water! I rushed out after eleven o'clock. A terrible sight. The furious torrents rolled from the mountains in the moonlight—fields, trees, and hedges torn up, and the entire valley one deep lake agitated by the roaring wind! And when the moon shone forth, and tinged the black clouds, and the wild torrent at my feet foamed and resounded in this grand and frightening light, I was overcome by feelings of terror, and at the same time yearning. With arms extended, I looked down into the yawning abyss, and cried, "Down! Down!" For a moment I was lost in the intense delight of ending my sorrows and my sufferings by a plunge into that gulf! But then I felt rooted to the earth and incapable of ending my woes! (69–70)

If only he could give himself over to this energy in sublime nature, to this wild torrent, the problem of the satisfaction of impossible desire would at least be ended, if not solved. Werther's itinerary lets itself be read as a move from sometime attachment to the beautiful to complete domination by the sublime, ending in the realization that only this end is possible. In some earlier scenes of the perception of nature, Werther's awareness shifts abruptly and jarringly back and forth between a sense of the "overflowing fullness" of nature, before which he feels "as if a god myself," and a sense of nature as "an all-consuming, devouring monster" (36–37). At this late moment in December, he remains in the condition he had earlier ascribed to humanity in general: "we are as poor and limited as ever, and our soul still languishes for unattainable happiness" (20). His death looms, but he does yet quite grasp it: "My hour is not yet come: I feel it" (70).

Werther's relations to Lotte directly mirror his relations to nature. Both are dominated by his hyperbolizing imagination, as he sees her now as beautiful, now as sublime. When he first sees her, he finds

six children, from eleven to two years old . . . running about the room, surrounding a lovely girl of medium height, dressed in a simple white frock with pink ribbons. She was holding a loaf of dark bread in her hands, and was cutting slices for the little ones all round, in proportion to their age and appetite. She performed her task with such affection, and each child awaited his turn with outstretched hands and artlessly shouted his thanks. (15)

Everything here is simple, cozy, natural, and artless, in forming a scene of mildness with which Werther would like to identify. But then he also dreams that "I pressed her to me and covered with countless kisses those dear lips of hers which murmured words of love in response. Our eyes were one in the bliss of ecstasy" (70). There is scarcely a better case than this of a fantasized, impossible specular moment.

In each case, Lotte is more a posited object of Werther's fevered imagination of himself in relation to her than she is seen by him as a being in her own right. She is an occasion for him to fantasize himself complete, both original and at home. Lotte here plays the same role as was played by the earlier object of his affections, whom Werther describes wholly in terms of her effect on him: "I have felt that heart, that noble soul, in whose presence I seemed to be more than I really was, because I was all that I could be. God! Was there a single power in my soul that remained unused? And in her presence could I not develop fully that intense feeling with which my heart embraces Nature?" (8). Here, as ever, the real object of Werther's consciousness is *my soul, my heart, my seeming to be more than I really was.* No wonder, then, that when he imagines that she loves him, Werther rhapsodizes in the same egocentric terms: "That she loves me! How the idea exalts me in my own eyes! And . . . how I worship myself since she loves me!" (27).

Werther's self-claimed exceptionalism, his sense that, unlike in ordinary people, "there lie dormant within me so many other qualities which wither unused, and which I must carefully conceal" (8), leads him consistently to scorn ordinary life and the achievements of reciprocity, decency, and human relationship that are possible in it. In

particular, he scorns, while also envying, Albert's staid conventional-
ism and decency. But he here finds Albert only to be typical of what
most people are like. "Most people," he writes, "work the greater part
of their time just for a living; and the little freedom which remains
to them frightens them, so that they use every means of getting rid
of it. Such is man's high calling!" (8). In contrast, Werther seeks for
himself a genuine high calling and exemplary, commanding achievement outside the framework of the ordinary. Not for him "the gilded
wretchedness, the boredom among the silly people who parade about
in society here" (44) at court, a world in which he stands as if "before
a puppet show and see[s] the little puppets move . . . completely oc-
cupied with etiquette and ceremony" (45). Unable to mix with them,
he argues that real love, constancy, and passion "exists in its greatest
purity among that class of people whom we call rude, uneducated"
(55), as he again hyperbolically idealizes a pastoralized ordinary life.
Yet he is unable, with his dormant qualities he must carefully conceal lest he subject them to the risks of public scrutiny, to mix with
ordinary people either.

Work, too, is treated by Werther as something either stalely conventional and meaningless or idealized as salvific. On the one hand,
"the man who, purely for the sake of others, and without any passion or inner compulsion of his own, toils after wealth or dignity, or
any other phantom, is simply a fool" (28). On the other hand, "Many
a time I wish I were a common laborer, so that when I awake in the
morning I might at least have one clear prospect, one pursuit, one
hope, for the day which has dawned" (37). In both cases, his attention is on the work as the vehicle of the exalted expression of his
personality, not on the work itself and those who do it. Even when
he imagines doing a small bit of work in first arriving at the court
of Count C., his thoughts remain on himself and his superiority to
others. "But when, in spite of weakness and disappointments, we do
our daily work in earnest, we shall find that with all false starts and
compromises we make better headway than others who have wind
and tide with them; and it gives one a real feeling of self to keep
pace with others or outstrip them in the race" (42).

Werther's God is similarly exceptional—a being whom he assumes either specifically listens to his pleas or specifically avoids them, without any mediating institutions or any involvements in the lives of others. On November 30, as he approaches his end, he addresses God directly and intimately, presuming to be his particular and special son.

> Father, Whom I know not—Who were once wont to fill my soul, but Who now hidest Thy face from me—call me back to Thee; be silent no longer! Thy silence cannot sustain a soul which thirsts after Thee. What man, what father, could be angry with a son for returning to him unexpectedly, for embracing him and exclaiming, "Here I am again, my father! Forgive me if I have shortened my journey to return before the appointed time. The world is everywhere the same—for labor and pain, pleasure and reward, but what does it all avail? I am happy only where thou art, and in thy presence I am content to suffer or enjoy." And Thou, Heavenly Father, wouldst Thou turn such a child from Thee? (64)

His address here is strikingly reminiscent of his earlier thoughts about Lotte, whom he similarly regards as his unique savior. "I cannot pray except to her. My imagination sees nothing but her; nothing matters except what has to do with her" (38).

What does it all avail? Seeking absolute and perfect ratification of his exceptional personality and talents and perfect, autonomous selfhood joined to continuing sociality in a life of daily self-affirming divinity but finding only ordinary people and his own tortured thoughts and fantasies, Werther can in the end hit only on the strategy of giving it all up. The only freedom from continuing failure is death. "We desire to surrender our whole being" (20), and if partial, egocentric surrender to Lotte, to art, to nature, or to work is received and ratified by no one, ordinary as they all are, then genuine surrender must be complete, an escape from life itself. "I have heard of a noble race of horses that instinctively bite open a vein when they are hot and exhausted by a long run, in order to breathe more freely. I am often tempted to open a vein, to gain everlasting liberty for myself" (50). As he recalls almost kissing Lotte, "And yet I want—but it stands like a barrier before my soul—this bliss—and then die to expiate the sin! Is it sin?" (62). In the end, "The body was carried by workmen. No clergymen attended" (87).

Goethe himself, of course, did not commit suicide, despite the autobiographical character of the novel. Mann suggests that Goethe's willingness to go on living had to do with his sense of his identity as a writer. "Goethe did not kill himself," Mann writes, "because he had *Werther*—and quite a few other things—to write. Werther has no other calling on this earth except his existential suffering, the tragic perspicacity for his imperfections, the Hamlet-like loathing of knowledge that suffocates him: thus he must perish."[17] How did Goethe then come to have and to be aware of having another calling, one that made life for him worth living? As Mann suggests, the answer has to do with the very act of writing *Werther*, as well as with the ongoing activity of writing for a public already begun with *Goetz von Berlichingen*. For Goethe, the act of writing in general, and of writing *Werther* in particular, combined a kind of catharsis—both a clarification and an unburdening—of his emotional life with the achievement of a kind of distance or perspective on himself. He came through writing to achieve a sense of himself as having a social identity as a writer, so that the problem of wedding autonomous selfhood to continuing sociality did not for him go fully unsolved. It would be addressed again and again in the act of writing, from *Faust* to the lyric poetry to *Elective Affinities*, though with more maturity and never quite perhaps with the immediate cathartic intensity of address of *Werther*. Yet even in his maturity Goethe retained an intense subjectivity capable of responding to others as though they were vehicles of salvation for him. Mann notes that at the age of seventy-two he fell in love with the seventeen-year-old Ulrike Sophie von Levetzow. Though address and partial solution to the problem of subjectivity are possible, full solution is not.

Ludwig Wittgenstein's character strongly resembles those of Goethe and Werther. Both his personal and philosophical writings combine an intense wish for attachment to others and to activities as vehicles for the expression of the higher self he felt himself to have with an equally intense critical scrutiny of that wish. The subtitle of Ray Monk's biography, *The Duty of Genius*, captures this feature of his character well. For the young Wittgenstein in particular, the realization and confirmation of genius was, in Monk's words, "a Categorical Imperative," and the only alternative to failing to follow it was death: genius or suicide. "Wittgenstein's recurring thoughts of suicide between 1903 and 1912, and the fact that these thoughts abated only after Russell's recognition of his genius, suggest that he accepted this imperative in all its terrifying severity."[18]

Monk traces Wittgenstein's submission to this imperative to his reading of Otto Weininger's *Sex and Character*, published in 1903, the year of Weininger's own suicide. Brian McGuinness accepts this connection but goes further to read this imperative into the composition of the *Tractatus* and to situate it in the context of Wittgenstein's family life and surrounding culture. McGuinness characterizes what he calls "the final message of the *Tractatus*" as "perhaps a clearer, a more concentrated view . . . would enable him to see the world aright. At any rate, if there was no real prospect of this: if he could not reach this insight, and if he could not get rid of his troubles by reconciling himself to the world, then his life was pointless."[19] What made this question—genius or suicide—arise with special force in Wittgenstein's case, McGuinness argues, was not only the example and influence of Weininger or the general sickness of prewar Austrian culture but also and more deeply the influence on him of his father. The Wittgenstein family

> formed a sort of enclave, fortified against the corruption and inadequacy that surrounded it by severe and private moral standards, which, it seemed, some of them had not the tem-

perament to match or meet. Ludwig's case . . . seems to have been that of a phenomenally strong assent and attachment to these standards, often at war not only with the normal human failings that became glaring in their light, but also with a particularly soft and affectionate nature.[20]

Yet McGuinness immediately goes on to add that Wittgenstein himself "was not one to see his problem as that of being unable to do what his father required,"[21] and he further comments that "what we are describing here is no disease. As Tolstoy says: 'These questions are the simplest in the world. From the stupid child to the wisest old man, they are in the soul of every human being.'"[22] With the example of *Werther* before us, we can see the problem of genius or suicide as forming a strong theme in German culture in its response to the yet more general problem in modernity of wedding autonomous selfhood to continuing sociality.

Wittgenstein's preoccupation with autonomy and with the realization and confirmation of genius against the grain of culture is pronounced in the remarks in his own voice published as *Vermischte Bemerkungen* (*Culture and Value*). "It's a good thing," he writes, "I don't allow myself to be influenced."[23] As is typical in the post-Kantian, post-Goethean German tradition, the realization of genius is conceived of as a matter of letting something natural and divine come to the fore in one's thought and life, often under the prompting of nature itself. "Just let nature speak and acknowledge only *one* thing as higher than nature, but not what others may think" (1e). "Don't take the example of others as your guide, but nature!" (41e).

When one is thus guided, one's thinking and acting happen with significance, in and through one, rather than under one's personal control. "One might say: art *shows* us the miracles of nature. It is based on the *concept of the miracles of nature*. (The blossom, just opening out. What is *marvellous* about it?) We say: 'Just look at it opening out!'" (56e). It is just this kind of natural yet significant opening out of his own features of character that Wittgenstein anxiously hoped might inform his own thinking and writing.

Schiller writes of a "poetic mood." I think I know what he means, I believe I am familiar with it myself. It is a mood of receptivity to nature in which one's thought seems as vivid as nature itself. . . . I am not entirely convinced that what *I* produce in such a mood is really worth anything. It may be that what gives my thoughts their lustre on these occasions is a light shining on them from behind. That they do not *themselves* glow. (65e–66e)

Something hidden, powerful, and natural within oneself is to come to the fore, in a way that is not under one's egocentric control. One is to be swept along by one's genius into a natural-supernatural movement of thinking.

Yet talent can also be betrayed or misused, and so fail to confirm itself in its products. "Talent is a spring from which fresh water is constantly flowing. But this spring loses its value if it is not used in the right way" (10e). As a result, the most important thing is to come to think and write naturally, in faithfulness to one's talent and against the grain of culture. But the effort to do so takes place within the conventionalized space of personally controlled and discursive reflection, so that it is crossed by an anxious self-scrutiny. "Am I thinking and writing as it were beyond myself, out of the depths of the natural?" one egocentrically and discursively wonders, or Wittgenstein wonders, in just the sort of tragic obsessiveness about his own imperfections that Mann saw in Werther. "Working in philosophy . . . is really more a working on oneself. On one's own interpretation. On one's way of seeing things. (And what one expects of them.)" (16e). "No one *can* speak the truth; if he has still not mastered himself. He *cannot* speak it;—but not because he is not clever enough yet. The truth can be spoken only by someone who is already *at home* in it; not by someone who still lives in falsehood and reaches out from falsehood towards truth on just one occasion" (35e). All or nothing; natural-supernatural, nonconventionalized, poetic truth and expressiveness or imitative, derivative, nonexistence; genius or suicide.

Domination by this imperative produces the same complex of attitudes toward work and toward religion that we find in Werther. On the one hand, Wittgenstein idealizes ordinary manual work as something beautiful and honest, more honest than intellectual chatter: "what is ordinary is here filled with significance" (52e),[24] if the manual work is done with respect and integrity. It is no accident, but rather deeply part of his anxious self-scrutiny and his attitudes toward culture and value, that Wittgenstein so often urged others to take up this kind of work. On the other hand, "Genius is what makes us forget skill" (43e). It is beyond the ordinary. So how can one express genius within the framework of the ordinary? How can one write poetically—originally and yet in a way that draws on the common and is accessible to others? How can one wed autonomous selfhood to continuing sociality? "I think I summed up my attitude toward philosophy when I said: philosophy ought really to be written only as a *poetic composition*. . . . I was thereby revealing myself as someone who cannot quite do what he would like to be able to do" (24e).

Religious faithfulness offers a paradigm of significant expressiveness, but it is a paradigm that in its traditional, institutionalized form is dead for us, shot through with the conventionality that expressiveness is to overcome. "What is good is also divine. Queer as it sounds, that sums up my ethics. Only something supernatural can express the Supernatural" (3e). What is needed is "a light from above" that comes to the individual soul, not religious institutions and ordinary religious training. "Is what I am doing really worth the effort? Yes, but only if a light shines on it from above. . . . And if the light from above is lacking, I can't in any case be more than clever" (57e–58e). Religious belief cannot be something that is simply given and shared. It must rather be achieved through the dormant qualities of one's soul coming actively to take religious life as the vehicle of their expression, as providing the terms of deep significance. "It strikes me that a religious belief could only be something like a passionate commitment to a system of reference. Hence, although it's a *belief*, it's really a way of living, or a way of assessing life. It's passionately seizing hold of *this* interpretation" (64e).

Above all, what Wittgenstein wants from religion, from work, from the guidance of nature, from his genius, but can never quite find, is full-blooded and continuing significance in the face of mere conventionality and cleverness: a new life. "A confession has to be part of your new life" (183). And if not a new life, then death: genius or suicide, or suicide as the creative act of voluntarily removing oneself from a cycle of unending self-defeat. In 1946, in the middle of remarks about music, thought, Shakespeare, God, heroism, and the difficulty of philosophy, there occurs in *Culture and Value*, in quotation marks, the very last words of Werther to his correspondent Wilhelm: "Lebt wohl!"[25]

The intensities of Wittgenstein's character have been well documented in the biographical literature. Yet one might argue that these intensities have little to do with his actual philosophical thinking and writing, or at least with what he chose to have published. After all, as he also wrote in *Culture and Value*, "My ideal is a certain coolness. A temple providing a setting for the passions without meddling with them" (2e). Yet it would be striking were his official philosophical writing to be wholly uninformed by the otherwise deepest preoccupations of his character. Even in this remark, he presents *a certain coolness* as an ideal, not as something that he has actually achieved, and he did note that he was "someone who cannot quite do what he would like to be able to do" (24e). Is *Philosophical Investigations* in any sense *about* the problem of the realization of talent against the grain of but always in relation to the affordances of culture and the ordinary, *about* the problem of wedding autonomous selfhood to continuing sociality? That *Philosophical Investigations* is about this, in detail, line by line, as well as being about the nature of meaning, understanding, the will, and so on, and about this *by* being about these latter topics, is a main line of argument of my *Leading a Human Life: Wittgenstein, Intentionality, and Romanticism*. I cannot recapitulate the whole of that argument here. But I will offer a few brief pointers to it.

In section 125 of *Philosophical Investigations*, we find that "das philosophische Problem . . . ist . . . die bürgerliche Stellung des Widerspruchs, oder seine Stellung in der bürgerlichen Welt"; in English, and appropriately, that "the philosophical problem . . . is . . . the civil status of a contradiction, or its status in civil life."[26] "Our entanglement in our rules is what we want to understand" (§125). This entanglement "throws light on our concept of *meaning* something" (§125). What is it to be entangled in rules in civil life, in ordinary life, in the ordinary, civil *bürgerlichen* world? Not to "know one's way about" (§123) is not to know how to engage with this world, not to know how to bring one's talents and selfhood to authentic, nonderivative, and yet ratifiable expression within it. To ask "what does this knowledge [of how to go on in applying a rule] consist in?" (§148) is to ask what there is in me—what talent, what locus of understanding, what source of mastery—that enables me to go on and *how* to bring this talent, locus, or source to apt expression. Something must be there in me. I can do something, and we are not in using language either machines or other animals. But what is it? And do I bring whatever it is to expression aptly? How? I seem caught between an anxiety that the only routes of expression are those already laid down in surrounding practice, that I contribute nothing, that I am ordinary, and hence nonexistent: call this the anxiety of expressibility, and an anxiety that I cannot express that whatever-it-is in the ordinary, that I am alone, and mad: call this the anxiety of inexpressibility. To be able to mean something, to understand something: these are the results of the mysterious engagement of spontaneity in me, the source of originality, with the routes of expression that are given in practice, as though a seed in me—but one I can never identify or cultivate deliberately—grew in relation to its environment. "Each morning you have to break through the dead rubble afresh so as to reach the living warm seed. A new word is like a fresh seed sewn on the ground of the discussion" (2e). It may well be that there is for the language user "a special experience" of understanding, but this special experience cannot be grasped and deliberately deployed independently of engagement with the affordances of culture. "For us it is the *circumstances* under which he had such an experience that justify him in saying in such a case that he understands, that he knows how to go on" (§155). The always mysterious interaction of circumstances, that is, of the affordances of culture in providing routes of expression, with the powers of selfhood is something to be accepted, not explained in either a scientific or intellectualistic theory.

Wittgenstein too, like Goethe but unlike Werther, did not commit suicide. His last words, famously, were "Tell them I've had a wonderful life."[27] Like Goethe, he achieved through the act of writing, repeatedly and day to day, a kind of catharsis, *some* distance or perspective on his anxieties as a subject and some sense of himself as having a social identity as a writer. Hence there is some point to thinking that the second voice of the *Investigations* (if there are only two)—the voice that rebukes the tendency to seek scientific or intellectualist explanations of our cognitive abilities and that recalls us instead to the ways of the ordinary—*is* Wittgenstein's more mature voice. At the same time, however, the first voice—the voice of temptation and of intensities of perfect explanation and attunement—is his too, a voice he cannot quite give up, much as Goethe in his maturity would not give up intensities of infatuation and would still also identify himself with such intensities in Edward in *Elective Affinities*. The mature voice of the ordinary, the voice of survival, comes to the fore and is allowed the last word within a section, but always in continuing critical engagement with the voice of perfectly grounded and explained attunement, the voice of temptation.

Wittgenstein knew all this about himself. In 1931, in one of the remarks of *Culture and Value*, he wrote: "The delight I take in my thoughts is delight in my own strange life. Is this joy of living?" (22e). It is hard to tell. There is, once again, an all too present threat of narcissism in self-delight in thinking, in 1931 as in 1774. But it is also self-defeating simply to accommodate to the ordinary as it stands, eschewing thinking about better possibilities of life. By 1931, the idea that joy might be found in the activity of thinking one's own thoughts appears more a modernist or late romantic question in the face of increasing social fractures than as a first-generation romantic prayer and conjecture. If human being is the kind of being that can call its own being into question, that can think about life otherwise, exactly how it is to do this and with what prospects of fuller common life are, in the twentieth century, far from clear. To ask this question, and to write out this asking, again and again, is one powerful, anxious modernist face of the continued courting of responsiveness and responsibility, of the continued courting of the life of a subject.

4.

Attention, Expressive Power, and Interest in Life

Wordsworth's "Tintern Abbey"

I

In the first sentence of section 1 of *The Birth of Tragedy*, Nietzsche urges us to think about art in relation to life in a new way: "We shall have gained much for the science of aesthetics, once we perceive not merely by logical inference, but with the immediate certainty of vision, that the continuous development of art is bound up with the *Apollinian* and *Dionysian* duality—just as procreation depends on the duality of the sexes, involving perpetual strife with only periodically intervening reconciliations."[1] This claim forces us to ask two sets of questions.

(1) What is the vision of the development of art as bound up with this duality opposed to? That is, what other way of looking at art in relation to life are we being asked to give up? And how is what we are to see anew—the continuous development of art—like the development of humanity through procreation? The answers to these questions must involve the thought that the development of art does not come to an end just as the development of the human species does not come to an end: both developments are continuing and embodied in

essentially varying particulars. This fact makes otiose, then, the idea that the nature of art could be adequately and usefully described in a definition that specifies necessary and sufficient conditions to which the ideal work fully conforms, for no ideal, perfect work is possible, any more than a single ideal human being is.[2] If no ideal work is possible, then there will always be imperfections in any particular work and questions about exactly how and how well it approximates the ideal. An ideal definition will be insufficient to settle such questions, and judgment and discernment will be called for. Just as women and men with their differences and peculiarities—and not any perfect single human being—produce further women and men with their differences and peculiarities, so works of art are produced by temporary couplings of two forces in us—the Apollinian and the Dionysian—that are never fully integrated and balanced to form a single perfect whole. To *see* this fate—a continuing failure to achieve the ideal and to overcome all difference, peculiarity, and opposition—*in* every work of art is then to be weaned from the pursuit of a standing philosophical *logos* or definition: *that* pursuit functions only to deny the movement of life. When Plato, for example, assigned poetry "the rank of *ancilla*" in relation to philosophy and its definitions, favoring only the "enhanced Aesopian fable" with a moral amenable to rational justification, he thereby shied away from both the genuine complex and disturbing powers of art and the genuine turbulence of life. With Plato, Nietzsche tells us, "the Apollinian tendency has withdrawn into the cocoon of logical schematism" and so given up on life, transformation, and development.[3] Nietzsche, in contrast, is asking us to look the ongoing turbulence of life full in the face: to *see* it *at work in* every work of art and every human life.

(2) But then how is a genuinely successful work of art possible at all? It must involve a creative coupling of the Apollinian and Dionysian forces or tendencies in us that figure in artistic making, yet success in this coupling is not assessable according to any fixed ideal or conceptual measuring stick. The various products and values that are, according to Nietzsche, typical of each of these tendencies can be roughly set out as follows:

APOLLINIAN	DIONYSIAN
Dreams	Intoxications
Created supplement to life	Chaotic essence of life
Sculpture	Music
Form-order	Passion, drive, content
Enjoyable illusions	Fusion in "feeling-with"
Composure-trance-absorption	*Ekstasis*
Culture, civilization	Nature
Upholding of *principium*	Collapse of *principium*
individuationis	*individuationis*

In *The Will to Power*, Nietzsche describes these tendencies further and repeats the analogy between artistic production and sexual reproduction.

> The word "Dionysian" means: an urge to unity, a reaching out beyond personality, the everyday, society, reality, across the abyss of transitoriness: a passionate overflowing into darker, fuller, more floating states . . .
> The word "Apollinian" means: the urge to perfect self-suf- ficiency, to the typical "individual," to all that simplifies, distin- guishes, makes strong, clear, unambiguous, typical: freedom under law.
> The further development of art is necessarily tied to these two natural artistic powers as the further development of man is to that between the sexes. Plenitude of power and moderation.[4]

These powers must then be jointly expressed in the successful work. This expression must involve something other than either simple fusion, which would leave these powers unrecognizable in their individuality and hence unexpressed, and simple juxtaposition, in which there would be no coupling, no productive interrelation. But then how is success in the joint expression of these powers pos- sible at all?

Nietzsche offers an answer not in the form of a definition or principle but in the invocation of an example—an example that remains central for him throughout his subsequent career—at the end of the first paragraph of *The Birth of Tragedy*: "this coupling ultimately generated an equally Dionysian and Apollinian form of art—Attic tragedy."[5] So how, then, did Attic tragedy succeed in expressing these forces in an exemplary way, albeit one that is not successfully imitable according to a rule? The key to answering this question lies in seeing that the Attic Greeks courageously accepted the chaotic onwardness of meaningless, self-proliferating biohistorical life and then formed coherent, recognizable, individual lives anyway. "The profound Hellene"—both certain central figures in Greek tragedies and the members of chorus and audience who see and respond to their actions—"uniquely susceptible to the tenderest and deepest suffering, comforts himself, having looked boldly right into the terrible destructiveness of so-called world history as well as the cruelty of nature."[6]

In accepting clearly the destructiveness and cruelty of human life in nature and history, the Hellene resembles Hamlet and, in turn, us—we for whom the consolations of a superintending logos or Providence story are gone.

> The Dionysian man resembles Hamlet: both have once looked truly into the essence of things, and they have *gained knowledge*, and nausea inhibits action; for their action could not change anything in the eternal nature of things; they feel it to be ridiculous or humiliating that they should be asked to set right a world that is out of joint. . . . An insight into the horrible truth outweighs any motive for action, both in Hamlet and the Dionysian man.[7]

For one who bears such an insight, it is unclear what, if anything, is to be done, in any way that matters. "Now no comfort avails any more; longing transcends a world after death, even the gods; existence is negated along with its glittering reflection in the gods or in an immortal beyond. Conscious of the truth he has once seen, man now sees everywhere only the horror or absurdity of existence."[8] And yet, somehow, the Hellene nonetheless "comforts himself." This comfort is achieved in two distinct ways. "The comic" enables "the artistic discharge of the nausea of absurdity." That is, there is a kind of purging of nausea in the Dionysian self-abandonment of laughter. And, second, there is "the sublime as the artistic taming of the horrible."[9] This artistic taming happens through the setting up of a fiction within which it is possible for a life within the chaos of nature nonetheless to take on coherent form. "The Greek built up the scaffolding of a fictitious *natural state* and on it placed fictitious *natural beings*."[10] The sublimity that attaches to these fictitious natural beings—the protagonists of tragic drama—is that they stand out in their coherence of personality, diction, thought, and action against the chaos of nature. Their lives have form. The imposition of artificial emplotment on and for these fictitious natural beings in this fictitious natural state requires the dramatist to "dispense from the beginning with a painstaking portrayal of reality,"[11] with all its meaningless incidents. What is presented is rather an account of how a protagonist intelligibly moves toward his fate in his circumstances, with "probability or necessity,"[12] as Aristotle says. The *hexis*, or character, of the protagonist, with its one-sidedness (*hamartia*) or excess of virtue that is ill-fit to the circumstances of action, intelligibly brings it about that a reversal (*peripeteia*) occurs, accompanied with recognition (*anagnoresis*) by the protagonist, the chorus, and the spectators of the intelligibility of the action.[13] Yet though it is a fiction, this world in which protagonists coherently have characters and reach their fates intelligibly "is no arbitrary world placed by whim between heaven and earth; rather it is a world with the same reality and credibility that Olympus with its inhabitants possessed for the believing Hellene."[14] This world is set up "for [the] chorus"[15] and for the audience whose responses it shapes and models. In this world, chorus and audience see that a character—a protagonist with a *hexis* or unified ensemble of powers of thought, reasoning, expression, and action—can impress that *hexis* on the world by expressing it in intelligible action, however ill-starred the outcome. In this way, the protagonist "lives anyway" for the chorus and audience, despite the meaningless of life "in itself" in nature and history "in themselves." Antigone and Oedipus, and Hamlet and Lear, are figures of sublime accomplishment, Nietzsche is arguing, in standing out for us intelligibly from the chaos of life in the coherence and power of their thought, diction, and action. They have lived as subjects of their lives, experiences, and actions rather than as mere things, in a way that is both exemplary and comforting for us.

II

On the surface, Wordsworth's tone is far more optimistic than Nietzsche's. The universe itself, he writes, "moves with light and life informed, / Actual, divine, and true,"[16] and we may find Paradise to be "A simple produce of the common day."[17] Yet such displays of felt metaphysical confidence are never either self-standing or stable. They are surrounded by narratives that describe recurrent movements through despair and recovery, and they are strongly qualified by being cast in the subjunctive mood or as expressions of hopes about future reception. Wordsworth typically *conjectures at a moment* both that he has so experienced nature and the human world in it and that others *may* experience them similarly, thus sanctifying his prophetic authority in matters of culture and value.[18] His major works conclude more typically with an expression of a hard won, prayerful hope that his vision will or may be taken up than with a confident pronouncement that that vision is true and proven. Put otherwise, his major poems are more records of experiences of thinking and feeling through which poetic identity and authority are *temporarily* achieved than they are pieces of straight metaphysical philosophy.

The underlying problem that motivates Wordsworth's continual swervings among expression of feeling, metaphysical pronouncement, conjectures about reception, and recurrent hesitancy and doubt is that of achieving life as a fully responsive and responsible human subject. Wordsworth seeks both to become a locus of feeling coupled with apt understanding and to find that achievement of fullness of subjectivity certified by others. Absent such certification, the achievement itself is open to doubt. For Wordsworth, the very idea that he has lived or can live *as a subject* is always threatening to falter, most memorably in the image of himself as one "Unprofitably traveling toward the grave, / Like a false steward who hath much received / And renders nothing back" that launches the *Prelude* on its course of self-interrogation.[19] When Wordsworth does at certain moments achieve a measure of confidence in his life and powers as a subject, he does so much more in the manner of the protagonists of tragic drama as Nietzsche understood them than in the manner of a theoretical philosopher. He manages, that is, recovery of himself *in time* through achieving a stably and powerfully enough formed manner of thought, expression, and (writerly) action, at least for a moment, in the face of the chaos of life, rather than simply reverting to metaphysical pantheism or any other epistemically well-founded doctrine or doxa. Fullness of responsiveness and responsibility are won, essentially at a moment, plausibly and in an exemplary way, thus overcoming passivity, drift, and despair for a time.

That there is a threat to the existence of life as a subject—a threat that dominates a great deal of contemporary life, but a threat that may be answered by the powers of poetry (not theoretical philosophy)—is the chief argument of the "Preface" to *Lyrical Ballads*. This argument is inaugurated as Wordsworth announces that "the principal object . . . proposed in these poems" is "above all, to make these incidents [and situations from common life] interesting,"[20] thus implying that common life is not interesting as it stands: we are dead to it and it to us. This implication is unpacked in the further thought that "a multitude of causes, unknown to former times, are now acting with a combined force to blunt the discriminating powers of the mind and, unfitting it for all voluntary exertion, to reduce it to a state of almost savage torpor" (449). Without the exercise of discriminating powers issuing in voluntary exertion—without fullness of responsiveness and responsibility—there is only more or less animal passivity in life, as one is buffeted about by circumstance, often compelled addictively to try to stop the pain of life by succumbing to a "degrading thirst after outrageous stimulation" (449). One fails to lead the life of an active subject moved by genuine interest.

Yet there is no hope that pure reasoning can save us. Wordsworth specifically eschews "the selfish and foolish hope of *reasoning* [the Reader] into approbation of these particular poems" insofar as it is not possible "to give a full account of the present state of public taste in this country, and to determine how far this taste is healthy or depraved" (445). That is to say, there is no account vouchsafed to us by reason or by anything else that determines what any ideal human life must be like, which account could serve as a standing measure of present life and taste. For that, we would need to know "in what manner language and the human mind act and re-act on each other" (446) in general and how "society" in its "revolutions" might play out these interactions well or badly. Such knowledge of standing conditions that would determine what counts as an ideal human life, fitly expressing distinctively human powers, is unavailable. We are too finite for that, with our reflections on our condition too shaped by our specific, sectarian particulars of personal and social history and place. Embodiment and the exercise of intelligence within it has, always, its localities.

To undertake to make the scenes and incidents of common life interesting but without any external measure of interest is then to aim to do the work of animation from within the having of ordinary experience. As Stanley Cavell puts it,

What the words "make interesting" say is that poetry is to make something happen—in a certain way—to the one to whom it speaks; something inside, if you like. That what is to happen to that one is that he or she is to become interested in something [is] . . . to perceive us as [at present] uninterested, in a condition of boredom, which [is regarded as], among other things, a sign of intellectual suicide.[21]

One must begin *from* the experience of common scenes and incidents, together with attendant thoughts and feelings. Then *within* courses of thoughts and feelings that are often clichéd, inattentive, or unanimated, one must *discover* or *uncover* those that are aptly attentive to the subject matter, so that one becomes animated as a subject in dwelling in just these aptly attentive thoughts and feelings. In this way one might hope, without an external standard, to "discover what is really important to men" so that "the understanding of the Reader must necessarily be in some degree enlightened, and his affections strengthened and purified" (448). The poet here acts as a kind of bootstrapping device for the achievement of animation from within ordinary experience that is otherwise dead, unattended to, and insignificant for us. It is for this reason that "the feeling therein developed gives importance to the action and situation, and not the action and situation to the feeling" (448). The proper work of poetry is not simply the depictive presentation of a subject matter but rather the working through of feeling in relation to a subject, so that genuineness of feeling is achieved. The poet here arrives at the aptness and fullness of response that must animate the life of a subject, if the subject is to find anything interesting at all. The poet "considers [man] as looking upon this complex scene of ideas and sensations, and finding every where objects that immediately excite in him sympathies which, from the necessities of his nature, are accompanied by an overbalance of enjoyment" (455). Here the enjoyment is no simple wash of sensory pleasure; it is rather a lingering in feeling as apt to the object of attention. Even when the scene attended to is horrible, one may have the sense that here, apart from the ordinary rush of hectic and inattentive life in which we are mostly caught up, one is feeling and responding fully and aptly, as an active subject, not a thing.

In this work of the animation of the life of a subject, the use of the self is crucial. Wordsworth notes that the poet's "own feelings are his stay and support; and, if he set them aside in one instance, he may be induced to repeat this act till his mind shall lose all confidence in itself and become utterly debilitated" (461–462). There is nothing to go on in beginning to aim at genuineness of feeling other than feeling as it already stands; nothing to go on to aim at fullness of life as a subject other than that life as it already exists, debilitated as it may be. One must find confidence in one's feelings from within them, even if they are at first cloudy and confused. Wordsworth tells us that he has "at all times endeavoured to look steadily at [his] subject" (450), where this effort at steadiness of looking includes a focus not only on the scene or incident at hand but also on himself as either debilitated or apt in his own course of feeling. The poet must ask himself: do my feeling and attention wander off into unsteadiness, absentmindedness, or unresponsive cliché, in relation either to the scene that initiates reflection or to the work of reflection on it? Am I, the poet asks, genuinely paying attention to the scene and to the work of reflection, in aptness of both thought and feeling? If, as may sometimes happen, the answer is yes, then the poet will be "a man pleased with his own passions and volitions, and who rejoices more than other men in the spirit of life that is in him" (453).

There is a considerable inherent risk of narcissism or of excessive self-satisfaction in taking upon oneself the role of the poet as a figure of exemplarity in thought and feeling. One might become *too* pleased too quickly in one's aptness of thought and feeling. This inherent risk is an aspect of the internalization of quest romance, of finding oneself to bear a problem of having to find routes of significant action from within one's own resources rather than from culture as it stands. This problem becomes increasingly pressing and difficult throughout the development of modernity, as diversity increases and fewer feelings and commitments are shared, absent willed fundamentalism.

For Wordsworth, awareness of the risk of narcissism continually haunts the work of the stabilization of attention and the work of writing. Doubts about whether one is genuinely thinking and feeling *as a subject* are inherent to the activity of seeking exemplarity in thought, feeling, and their expression. But if this risk is overcome and exemplarity is achieved, then the poet may arrive at "truth . . . carried alive into the heart by passion; truth which is its own testimony, which gives competence and confidence to the tribunal to which it appeals, and receives them from the same tribunal" (454). No other tribunal of aptness of feeling will serve. Instinct, tradition, fixities of form and craft, and proofs constructed by reason—these are all either unavailable or impotent to sanction the work of the achievement of aptness and genuineness of feeling and its expression.

Without this work—if we shy from it in anxiety, or under the conditions of modern economic life, or in simple distractedness of mind, or in reversion to what is comfortable enough as we all mostly do much of the time—subjects do not exist *as subjects*, as those who take *an interest in* their own experiences. They fail to live according to "the grand elementary principle of pleasure [in apt, genuine, and stable feeling], by which [man] knows, and feels, and lives, and moves" (455). As Wordsworth notes, no advances in science will make this work irrelevant. "If the labours of Men of science should ever create any material revolution, direct or indirect, in our condition, and in the impressions which we habitually receive, the Poet will sleep then no more than at present" (456). The work of the animation of life for us as subjects, the work of finding felt significance in scenes and incidents of common life, will continue to be necessary, no matter how the scenes and incidents of life themselves may change.

In this conception then, "the calling of poetry," as Cavell puts it, "is to give the world back, to bring it back, as to life."[22] The perception of the continuing need for this calling can be set out in a rough argument schema as follows:

(1) A person lives as a subject in a world of significance if and only if that person lives with attentive wholeheartedness, felt interest, and commitment in relation to objects of common experience.

(2) Mostly we do not live with attentive wholeheartedness, felt interest, and commitment in relation to objects of common experience.

Therefore

(3) Mostly we do not live as subjects in a world of significance.

One can of course reject the first premise. One might, in particular, wonder what sense can be made of the phrase "lives as a subject." Isn't it enough for that just to live—to be biologically alive—and simply to be a subject, that is, simply, say, to speak a language and to be aware of oneself as speaking it? Why should attentive wholeheartedness, felt interest, and commitment in relation to objects of common experience matter ontologically, as it were?

When, however, one is in the grip of the truth of the second premise, then the first premise seems all but inescapable, or at least Wordsworth in his thoughts about poetry registers a sense that it is for him inescapable. The issue is less naturalistically ontological than it is ethically ontological. We fail to exercise, or to exercise fully, defining powers that we possess and that we ought to exercise. Something is wrong with our present life, and that is just what premise 2 says in a specific way. When the thought that something in life is wrong is present for us, coupled with the thought that we can and should do better—should do something to remedy that wrong—then we are very close to accepting premise 1 as the expression of an ethical demand that (according to premise 2) we are failing to meet. The conclusion that we have arrived at a kind of ethical death-in-life is then itself all but inescapable. Mostly we do not live as subjects in a world of significance.

Poetry then seeks to overcome this conclusion by undertaking to reanimate our wholeheartedness, interest, and commitment in our lives and world from within the broken, half-hearted feelings we already have. No acquisition simply of information about the world will serve, for what is sought is significance in feeling, not an addition to a collection of facts. Nor will any life-denying escape from the world, say to a heaven of Platonic forms, avail us in coming to terms with this life. Instead, what Cavell more or less terms getting the hang of a posture—perhaps from reflection on feeling as it stands, perhaps also from picking up a precursor's routes of interest and expression—is what is called for. "You never know when someone will learn the posture, as for themselves, that will make sense of a field of movement, it may be writing, or dancing, or passing a ball, or sitting at a keyboard, or free associating. [A] sense of paradox expresses our not understanding how such learning happens."[23]

What is needed, then, is what Wordsworth cryptically calls the ability, possessed most typically by rural men, to "communicate with the best objects" (447). To communicate *with* objects (including persons and events) is not to communicate *about* them to others.[24] It is rather to arrive at a communion or intimacy with them, or a finding in feeling that one shares with them a life of significance. Only through such communion in meaningfulness is the life of a subject stabilized in the exercise of human powers.

David Wellbery has characterized this arrival at stabilization of the life of a subject as "the specular moment": "a perfect (and wordless) reciprocity between two selves"[25] or between a subject and a scene, object, or incident experienced as self-like. Such a wordless reciprocity is required to lift one out of circuits of decayed conventionality, exemplified in uses of language that are thoughtless, inattentive, or unfelt. Despite their saving graces, such specular moments are, Wellbery suggests, both sociohistorically contingent and ultimately uncapturable.[26] The need for and reversion to such moments arises typically or at least with special intensity in modernity, when other sources of stabilization are lacking, and typically or with special intensity for male subjects, caught up in routines of conventionalized work that they find meaningless and sealed off from an intimacy with nature that is stereotypically coded as feminine. Both women and nature are hence frequently forced to function as props for the male pursuit of the specular moment that is to stabilize anxious male selfhood. Even more troubling is the fact that specular moments themselves are transitory and subject to dispersion as soon as they become objects of explicit discursive awareness. To attend *to* them and to try to articulate their significance is to destroy them. As Wellbery puts it, "to render the specular moment in language is to submit it to an articulatory dismemberment and temporal deferral that fracture its essential unity."[27]

As a result, there is no possibility of arriving at a specular moment that is lasting, that possesses explicit, articulated significance, and that is innocent of a self-centered use of its object. But then there is no stabilization of the life of a subject without such moments either. The best, therefore, that one can do in seeking to certify that one is a (more) fully human subject as a locus of apt feeling, attention, and reflective-discursive awareness is to move through or in and out of such moments. A narrative of such movements will trace, always, an itinerary of both achievement and loss. The subject is undermined by temporality, discursiveness, and self-centeredness in the very moment of arrival at an evanescent stability and power. Any teachings that may be derived from such a moment will be conjectural and subject to immediate doubt. Yet there is, again, no other route to the perfection and stabilization of felt responsiveness to life out of conditions of empty materiality and ossified conventionality in which distinctively human powers are mostly betrayed.

Wordsworth, somehow, knows all this. His moments of strongest self-stabilization as a distinctive and exemplary human subject, apt in responsiveness to life and in thus achieving the life of a subject, are at the same time immediately subjected to doubt, and his itinerary of self-constitution fails to reach a fully stable end. One can hear a distinctive, honest, Wordsworthian hesitation even in the moments of most forceful conclusion. In the *Prelude*, Wordsworth announces that he and Coleridge will be

> Rich in true happiness if allowed to be
> Faithful alike in forwarding a day
> Of firmer trust, joint labourers in the work
> (Should Providence such grace to us vouchsafe)
> Of their deliverance, surely yet to come.[28]

"*If* allowed to be faithful . . . *should* Providence such grace to us vouchsafe"—it may not happen; the ways of the world as they stand may be too strong. Though the deliverance of humanity is "surely yet to come," the "surely" hints at an effort here too at self-reassurance. It may not come: Wordsworth did not write "Of their happy deliverance yet to come," which would scan about as well. In the "Preface," Wordsworth tells us that when he thinks about the ability of his and Coleridge's poetic writing to have any significant effect under the present degraded conditions of life,

> I should be oppressed with no dishonourable melancholy, had I not a deep impression of certain inherent and indestructible powers of the human mind, and likewise of certain powers in the great and permanent objects that act upon it, which are equally inherent and indestructible; and were there not added to this impression a belief, that the time is approaching when the evil will be systematically opposed, by men of greater powers, and with far more distinguished success. (449)

For all the confidence that it expresses, this passage also says that melancholy may not be dishonorable. The only blocks against it are certain impressions, but where are they to be found, how lasting can they be, and what joint work will they support, under present conditions? What if the work of attention and feeling that these poems invite is not in fact taken up by others?

Yet Wordsworth does not embrace melancholy, nor does he simply acquiesce in present conditions. Instead he goes on in the endless and endlessly self-scrutinizing work of pursuing life-enabling specular moments, articulating them (and thus betraying them), and coming to terms with human life in time, with all its movements of both self-stabilization and self-undoing.

David Miall has usefully called attention to the difference between typical locodescriptive poetry of the picturesque and Wordsworth's writing about his experience of nature. Where locodescriptive poetry focuses on what is seen, Wordsworth in contrast distinctively describes not so much what he sees as himself in the process of seeing. Miall develops this point by commenting on a fragment from Wordsworth's Alfoxden Notebook.

> To gaze
> On that green hill and on those scattered trees

> And feel a pleasant consciousness of life
> In the [?impression] of that loveliness
> Untill the sweet sensation called the mind
> Into itself by image from without
> Unvisited: and all her reflex powers
> Wrapp'd in a still dream forgetfulness
> I lived without the knowledge that I lived
> Then by those beauteous forms brought back again
> To lose myself again as if my life .
> Did ebb & flow with a strange mystery.[29]

As Miall notes, traditional readings of Wordsworth would focus here only on the moment of restoration, on how "the sweet sensation" of the natural scene "called the mind into itself." More recent New Historicist readings would argue that "the vision of unmediated benefit from Nature that the poem famously provides is, in this view, only a screen on which Wordsworth projects his anxieties."[30] But Miall calls our attention instead to the process, jointly of attention and of composition (of the poem and of the human subject), on display here. Wordsworth knows, and says, that his life "did ebb & flow with a strange mystery." Moments of (recuperative) self-loss are crossed with moments of (discursive) self-awareness; the movement between these moments is all.

Perhaps Stanley Cavell had something like this fact about Wordsworth (and Coleridge and Emerson and Thoreau) in mind when he remarked that "Romantics are brave in noting the possibility . . . of what you might call death-in-life. My favorite romantics are the ones (I think the bravest ones) who do not attempt to escape these conditions by taking revenge on existence. But this means willing to continue to be born, to be natal, hence mortal."[31] "To continue to be born" means here to eschew fundamentalisms involving the submission of the self to something apart from earthly life (Platonic forms or sacred texts, as may be) but also to eschew mere acquiescence and accommodation to a life of conventionalized getting and spending. Instead, movement both into and out of (Apollinian) moments of articulation and (Dionysian) moments of recuperative self-undoing is what is proper to the life of subject.

III

No matter what their theoretical desirability as both conditions of and contributions to life, whether such movements are possible—whether romantic bravery is possible—and what sort of closure or conclusiveness (without denying temporality) such movements might achieve are no small questions. That such movements are possible, and that measures of human closure and composure are available, within time and without denying life, are, I suggest, the central showings of "Tintern Abbey." Rather than either a document that (only, merely) traces the saving influence of nature or that (only, merely) shows a consciousness always in anxiety about its reception and unable to compose itself, "Tintern Abbey" shows a consciousness achieving a measure of composure in time, without intellectual certainties. It points to and exemplifies a path between dogmatism and nomadism, intellectual and moral alike. It can help us to hear "Tintern Abbey'''s showings if we divide its progress into eight rough stages of subject matter (thought) and attitude.

(1) "Five years have past; five summers, with the length / Of five long winters!" (1–2) [lines 1–22].[32] With these opening lines, the question of the meaning of life in time is raised. The apposition of the more subjective "five summers, with the length of five long winters!" (with subjectivity registered in both the felt succession of the seasons and in the sense that the winters have been long) to the more objective "five years" asks, already, what has the passing of these years meant in the life of a subject, in my life? The "and again I hear" that immediately follows introduces explicitly the I who is the subject of these reflections, an I that is wondering what its experience has meant. It has been suggested that the underlying subject and cause of this experience of questioning the meaning of some times of one's life are Wordsworth's guilt and anxiety over his evasion of the English military draft and over his affair and child with

Annette Vallon.[33] There may be some truth in this suggestion. The complex act of writing "Tintern Abbey" may well have occasioning circumstances that are rooted in the poet's past and that lie well outside the present scene alone. But whatever the occasioning circumstances may be, there is for us a question about whether the poem does any productive work in questioning the meaning of life in time. Any life will contain enough missteps and occasions for guilt and regret to prompt the raising of this question at some point. When one is in the grip of the thought that one is mostly living in half-heartedness and so failing to live as a full subject, then the question will be both natural and forward looking. What might I, or we, do in order to live with more wholeheartedness? Given the naturalness of this question at some point in any human life, it may repay our efforts if we attend to the work of the poem in its attempts to come to terms with it, without reversion to fundamentalism and without escapism. Perhaps these attempts are not even wholly successful. But we shall scarcely be able to see that before we engage with the work that the poem undertakes.

It has also been suggested that the move into the register of subjectivity, into the questioning of the meaning of a single subject's experience, more generally enacts a flight from the political.[34] This suggestion too may well bear some truth. But whether it does depends in large measure on what sort of politics we have in mind. Here we should not shrink from engaging with "Tintern Abbey"'s effort to find or found its own politics, that is, its own vision of a fuller, more human life in practice and in time. That vision does not have the shape of urging us toward either electoral politics or class struggle. But it is surely in part a vision of a better, more human polis. The topic, after all, is what it would be to lead the life of a subject, with others, under present conditions and in time.

To say "and again I hear these waters" after "five summers, with the length / Of five long winters" is to raise the question of repetition. Are we fated to it? And what does it mean that one finds oneself again stopped or halted in a place, in a moment of reflection? That death is all but explicitly on the poet's mind as he raises the question of the significance of life is suggested in the thought that "The day is come when I again repose / Here, under this dark sycamore" (9–10). "Repose" is stronger, more suggestive of permanence, than "recline," and "dark" suggests that one is in an enduring shade. To repose under this dark sycamore is almost to be under the ground. Though the poet goes on immediately to note that he views the present scene (and so is not dead, or not yet), nonetheless the thought that the day of a final repose will come is somewhere active in his consciousness of his place in relation to the scene before him. The thought of death is further echoed in the line "The Hermit sits alone" that, set apart by a line break, concludes this subject. With this Hermit, already a creature of the poet's imagination, not of perception alone, and with his isolation—with his lack of audience and companions, and so perhaps his insignificance—the poet may be taken to feel more than a little identification. With such apartness, what life? What doth life in time avail?

Consciousness of temporality is then further registered, both semantically and in internal citation, in the two instances of "Once again" (4, 14) that introduce the sentences surrounding the thought about repose. What has happened in the five years before these once agains, and what, if anything, does what has happened mean? What has filled and what should fill the passing of time? In raising this question, the poet does not turn for either knowledge or salvation to any exterior entities. Instead, as Miall cannily argues, he observes himself observing, and he invites us into his own jointly perceptive and apperceptive processes of consciousness of the present scene. In particular, in commenting on the phrase "hedgerows, hardly hedgerows" (15), Miall notes that

in the order of his phrases he recreates the *process* of observation: conventional, or schematic expectation would first look for hedgerows and find them; yet, a second glance—"hardly hedgerows"—would show the hedges in fact to be running wild. These lines thus invite the reader to replicate Wordsworth's own process of observation, a feature of several other elements in the opening paragraph. An object ("plots of cottage ground"; "pastoral farms") is first named, as an objective component of the scene, or what is to be expected in such a location (perhaps what was remembered from 1793); but it is then qualified in ways that suggest a second more careful focus on the actual details before him.[35]

The focus then is on how apperceptive awareness—awareness of oneself as observing and thinking in relation to this scene—may develop itself and on what assurances of possibilities of meaningfulness it may discover. This is, as Miall further notes, in strong contrast to typical locodescriptive poetry that takes as its central subject the scene itself rather than the poet's awareness of his processes of awareness of the scene.

(2) "Such, perhaps, / As have no slight or trivial influence . . ." (31–2) [22–49]. Lines 22–49 have seemed to many readers to be one of two grand metaphysical centers of the poem. (The other is lines 85–111.) Within these lines the poet all but asserts that he has seen "into the life of things" (49) in such a way that "the heavy and the weary weight / Of all this unintelligible world, / Is lightened" (39–41). Yet it is crucial that the poet does not in fact simply assert these claims. The passage begins with the claim that he has in the past at times remembered these forms, first experienced five years ago. His characterization of the feelings he has had as a result of these rememberings is strongly qualified. Some of them may be "unremembered" (31)—an acknowledgment that the report of feelings had in the past may be as much present construction (perhaps driven by need and anxiety) as recovery of an actual past. Such feelings "perhaps" have "no slight or trivial influence" on our lives, but then perhaps their influence is only slight and trivial. To what "little, nameless, unremembered acts / Of kindness and of love" (34–35) have they led, and in what way? The poet arrives at no definite account in answer to this question, and his formulation concedes its relevance—to him and to us. How can and should a life be constructed on the basis of feelings that may be unremembered and perhaps of slight influence? While there is a move *toward* the redemption of life in

time in the mention of these feelings and their influences, that move is considerably less than definite and conclusive. The gift of insight "into the life of things" provided by these feelings is also conjectural. "Nor less, I trust, / To them I may have owed another gift, / Of aspect more sublime" (35–37)—"trust" not "say," "may" not "thus." Has this gift actually come, and if so, through what processes? With such gifts of such a provenance, what salvation? The very movement toward saving certainties remains a lingering in uncertainties. Apperceptive awareness of oneself as thinking and feeling (rather than full immersion in sense-experience without reflection) includes, always, the thought that one is in part constructing the experience, not simply taking in any salvific given. And with awareness of constructedness comes present doubt. Or, at any rate, all this—perception plus conjecture plus intimately present doubt, in sharp contrast to simple intake and assertion—lies within the process of this poetic subject's attendings.

(3) "If this / Be but a vain belief . . . " (49–50) [lines 49–65]. Given the nature of the doubts expressed in the second section, "vain" has here the force of both "empty" and "ego-centered": perhaps the beliefs about the gifts presented by past feeling are empty *because* merely constructed in fantasy by a needy subject. "The fretful stir / Unprofitable, and the fever of the world, / Have hung upon the beatings of my heart" (52–54). The feelings that result may be compensatory but vain reactions to this stir and fever; they may be empty, because untrustworthy to others, and so to oneself, in the face of the ways of the world. That there is a risk of escapism in turning to them is part of the poet's own movement of thought. Human powers are not exercised amid the stir unprofitable of the world—mostly we do not lead the lives of subjects in a world of significance—and if not there, then where might they be? The twice pronounced "How oft(en)" (50, 57) "have I turned to thee, / O sylvan Wye" (55–56) is *both* an exclamation of gratitude to the Wye for being restoratively there to turn to *and* a genuine question: how often have I forgotten the Wye? How often have I been myself caught up in the ways of the world? There is, after all, not much chance of a life with people apart from these ways. A life wholly apart would itself be the life of a Hermit, itself too a life of all

but death, without reciprocity, intimacy, or recognition, though perhaps with some rough ontological power of persistence and survival,
whatever the ways of the world may be. If "the picture of the mind revives again" (61) "with pleasing thoughts / That in this moment there
is life and food / For future years" (63–65), there remains nonetheless
a question about how much this food will be genuinely present and
available. It has not, not always, been present in the past, as the world
has had its ways, and the deliverances of feeling may, again, be vain.
So "here I stand" (62). Is my life justified: before myself, before others,
or before God? What is the meaning of life in time? What exercises of
what human powers might lend significance to a life in time? There is
survival, to be sure: "here I stand" again, after "five years have passed,"
so that whatever death-in-life I have succumbed to, that succumbing
has not been complete. There remain in me, at least latently, human
powers of feeling and reflection that might issue in expressive action,
and those powers are to some extent activated by the present scene:
hence the thought that life and food for future years are to be found
in them. Animation of and within the life of a subject is felt to be
possible. But whither doth it point? A specular moment of recovery,
submitted to apperceptive reflection and to expression in language,
is immediately undone by these submissions. And they are unavoidable. Wordsworth at his strongest characteristically mixes a sense of
survival and restoration with doubt and uncertainty, and this standing here with pleasing thoughts that may yet be vain and evanescent
("how oft?") shows Wordsworth at his strongest.

(4) "And so I dare to hope . . . " (65) [lines 65–85]. Given his unresolved uncertainties, the poet's "dare to hope" is more apt than
"claim to know." Daring and hope indicate willed resolution backed
by nothing more than the fact of survival as a subject who does *not*
know the best exercises of his human powers but has survived anyway. The object of the infinitive "hope" is not specified, unless we
read the "so" as "in this manner" or "thusly" (rather than "therefore"),
so that it refers back to the "there is life and food / For future years"
of lines 64–65. "To dare to hope" is, again, far from a confident assertion of a truth. The poet dares to hope, uncertainly, that he stands,

in a moment and with pleasing thoughts, but these deliverances of apperception are themselves less than apodictic. In this resolution to hope there may be some survival of a subject, but a subject whose substantial nature remains unknown to him as any kind of stable thing. Nor does he know what is commanded of him by his nature as a subject, what a fit life for a human subject would be. At best, the stance is that of book 2 of the *Prelude*: "I was left alone / Seeking the visible world, nor knowing why. / The props of my affections were removed, / And yet the building stood, as if sustained / By its own spirit!"[36] Neither parent nor nature nor the visible world is present to provide props or reassuring grounds for affections. Hence the affections—the commitments and passions that motivate action—may be called into question. Their source and their value remain mysterious. And the subject stands only "as if sustained / By its own spirit!" Given the predominant effort to find or found a better standing for the subject, one may well wonder how much sustenance, how much food for future years, is really to be found in this survival.

Even the survival itself is immediately called into question. In the very moment of standing and daring to hope, the poet acknowledges that he is "changed, no doubt, from what I was" (66). There is no persistent substantial something to which the willed survival of the subject is referred. The subject has emerged within time through a fall or procession into discursive consciousness and apperceptive awareness. Somehow—he knows not how—he has come to be aware of himself as thinking, feeling, and judging, with less naturalness and automatism than attach to the life of a prereflective subject. He is no longer "like a roe / [Who] bounded o'er the mountains, by the sides / Of the deep rivers, and the lonely streams / Wherever nature led" (67–70).

With the fall out of naturalness in affection and activity comes a pressing need for reassurance or grounding. The mysterious joint onsets of discursive consciousness and apperceptive awareness bring a sense of distance from activity and of consequent anxiety. Before these onsets, one does not even seek "the thing [one] loves" (72), for there is only immediate activity without reflection and without seeking. After these onsets, one lives with desires (*désir, Begierde*), where the object of desire is explicitly conceptualized by and present to reflection, in contrast with the earlier, lost, more animal life of appetite or need (*besoin, Bedürfnis*). (Compare the transition in book 2 of the *Republic* from the first pastoral, natural, innocent but inhuman city of pigs to the second human city of luxuries and feverishness and competition.) Self-consciousness is desire in general.[37] Before its emergence, the poet in his movements through the natural world "had no need of a remoter charm, / By thought supplied, nor any interest / Unborrowed from the eye" (81–83). But "that time is past" (83); once somehow fallen into discursive consciousness, apperceptive awareness, and desire, there is no possibility of any return to any more innocent state. The earlier condition of prereflective awareness that is prior to the emergence of self-consciousness and desire cannot even be described: "I cannot paint / What then I was" (75–76). The origins of discursive thought cannot be established: "Hard task, vain hope, to analyse the mind, / If each most obvious and particular thought, / Not in a mystical and idle sense, / But in the words of Reason deeply weighed, / Hath no beginning."[38] Yet the poet also immediately undertakes to say something about what it was like to live in appetite alone, immersed in naturalness and without any need for or access to the remoter charms supplied by thought. The only relevance of this admitted fiction, perhaps like the fiction in political theory of a state of nature, must be to provide some sense of a dim possibility of wholeness and healthy activity for a subject who remains caught up in partiality and the feverish ways of the world. As David Bromwich has noted, the odd description of the innocent, animal activities of boyhood as those of one who is "more like a man / Flying from something that he dreads, than one / Who sought the thing he loved" (69–71) makes most sense if it is taken to refer to Wordsworth's life from 1793 (five years past) until the present moment in 1798.[39] Whatever occasioning circumstances we may suppose to lie behind these dreads and flights, it remains the case that this description suggests a life of a self-conscious being (of a man rather than boy) that is a life of dreads and flights and not at all a life of assurance in activity or of attentive wholeheartedness, felt interest, and commitment in relation to the objects of common experience. In this circumstance, without a recovery of a decipherable origin and without guiding assurances drawn from knowledge of the ultimate substance of the world and life, to dare to hope—across changes and in the wake of dreads and flights—must be at best an *act* of resolution that remains haunted by internal uncertainties and instabilities.

(5) "For such loss, I would believe . . . " (87) [lines 85–111]. In this section of second resolution or standing, the subject again makes an effort to gather himself, to resolve his uncertainties about life through the use of his own powers, without appealing to exterior things. This effort is again simultaneously successful *en mésure* and haunted by uncertainties. "I would believe" registers both: "I will believe (so far as I can)" and "I would like to believe (but can not, not quite wholly)." In either case, this formulation is substantially weaker, less assertational, than "I do believe." Verbs of agency that would express this belief are implied but not stated. The poet will not faint, mourn, or murmur, that is, will not give way to these at least partly passive and induced responses to life. He will or would in contrast more actively do something, but exactly what he would do is not specified. He has learned to adopt an attitude—"to look on nature" in a certain way—that should support a certain course of wholehearted interest, commitment, and activity. But what that course is remains unspecified, and learning to look on nature is itself not stabilized or grounded in learning theoretically *that* nature is (really, ultimately) thus and so. The adoption of an attitude is not grounded in theoretical knowledge, nor can it be. This adoption must remain in the register of resolution, in the register of what one "would believe."

The adoption of this attitude is supported, we are told, by the fact that "I have felt / A presence that disturbs me with the joy / Of elevated thoughts" (93–95). There is, however, no explanation of either the source of this feeling in ultimate things or its aptness to them. It is responsive to "something far more deeply infused / Whose dwelling is the light of setting suns, / And the round ocean, and the living air, / And the blue sky, and in the mind of man" (96–99). But this something is not named as an object of theoretical knowledge. At best it can be called an impelling "motion and a spirit" (100). Whatever joy felt responsiveness to this motion and spirit brings, it also brings disturbance, in the thought that one has not, not yet, lived fully in resonance with this spirit and its motions; perhaps one cannot so live. Metaphysical confidence is implied—but only implied, not stated, and disturbance yielding to doubt is not banished.

The resolution that concludes this section is now explicitly in the mode of will, not knowledge. "Therefore am I still" (102) expresses a determined effort at self-stabilization, at lingering as a whole subject within the specular moment of meaningfulness. For at least this moment of feeling, the subject is stabilized enough in its responsive resoluteness to be a subject in resonance with a significant order and so capable of wholehearted interest, commitment, and activity. But it cannot last. The announcement that the subject is "well pleased to recognize / In nature and the language of the sense, / The anchor of my purest thoughts, the nurse, / The guide, the guardian of my heart, and soul / Of all my moral being" (107–111) is honest to the moment of feeling and of self-resolution. But this announcement undoes itself in the very moment of its articulation. To say that one is "well pleased" is to hint that there is at least a danger that one is pleasing oneself by constructing this experience and its felt significance, where this construction may be driven by the needs of the subject rather than by how things are. Hence this construction may be both ego centered and empty. Wordsworth's special courage in the explorations of his movements of consciousness is to register this possibility and all the uncertainty it entails, rather than to deny it in reversion to dogma.

(6) "Nor perchance / If I were not thus taught" (111–112) [lines 111–134]. And so the poet accepts the possibility of error. It may be that he has not been thus taught by nature, that his depth of feeling and his resolution to be a coherent, expressive, responsive subject may be vain constructions. The poet's response to this possibility again takes the form of a resolution crossed with an imperative. "Nor . . . should I the more / Suffer my genial spirits to decay" (111, 112–113) were this

the case. I will not suffer this, and it is best for me not to suffer this. Things would not go well (standing melancholy would be my lot) were I to do so. So I will not do so. I would not that it be so.

That Dorothy ("thou my dearest Friend" [115]) is present with him in this spot to confirm his feeling and to stabilize his resolution suggests to the poet some help with his plight. I should not suffer my genial spirits to decay because thou art with me. But exactly how does her presence help? It does not cancel the registers of resolution and imperative, does not transform these registers into confident assertion. Quite the contrary, it moves the poet's consciousness explicitly into the mode of prayer. "Oh! Yet a little while / May I behold in thee what I was once, / My dear, dear Sister! And this prayer I make . . . " 119–121). "May I behold," not "shall I behold"; let it be so *Deo volente*, not I know that it is so. Nor is contact with an originary naturalness, putatively exemplified by Dorothy, so easily established. It is not clear that the poet in fact beholds that naturalness now: "may I behold," not "do I behold" "in thee what I was once." As John Barrell has argued, Wordsworth's desperate effort to achieve self-composure without turning to anything external to his experience

> requires Dorothy to perform a double function in the ratification of his achievement of a transcendent subjectivity. First, he needs to believe that Dorothy will grow up and sober up, for by doing so she will naturalise and legitimise his own loss of immediate pleasure in nature. The transition she makes, from the language of the sense to that of intellect, will be an observable process, one which will recapitulate and historicise the transition Wordsworth has already made. But in the second place, the language of the sense, as presently employed by Dorothy, stands as a present and audible guarantee of the meanings of his own language of the intellect; it assures him of the secure foundation of his language in the language of the sense.[40]

Barrell goes on to argue, quite cogently, that the double function assigned to Dorothy is incoherent. She cannot both grow up into discursive consciousness and apperceptive awareness and remain immersed in naturalness. "Dorothy can perform these two functions [repetition of growth into self-consciousness plus an anchoring persistence in naturalness], only if her potential for intellectual growth is acknowledged, but only if, also, that potential is never actualized."[41] It makes no sense, however, to assign her a potential that is both actualized and never actualized.

In all this Barrell is quite correct. But the problem goes even deeper than the use of Dorothy, and the problem is, moreover, registered in the poem itself. The problem is that no transition from naturalness (appetite) to discursive subjectivity (desire) can be both historically accomplished *and* naturalized, in such a way that the transition takes place (there is a fall into discursivity and into exteriority to nature) while a continuing saving resonance to pure naturalness is maintained. This is no more possible for William than it is for Dorothy. This fact accounts for the persistence until the end of the poem of the now explicit mode of prayer. What may happen, *Deo volente*, and what would save one as a subject by bringing one continuously into a life of full meaningfulness, is something that can never be known to happen, something that cannot even be coherently imagined by us to happen. "This prayer I make" (121)—that Dorothy fulfill this incoherent requirement, and that the poet himself has blended transcendent natural meaningfulness with finite subjectivity—must remain a prayer, not an announcement of an accomplishment. When the poet makes this prayer "Knowing that Nature never did betray / The heart that loves her" (122–123), the syntax undermines the claim to knowledge. "Never did" suggests an event of doubt, a fall into discursivity, apperceptive awareness, and exteriority to nature, a fall out of mere naturalness.[42]

It is no accident then that the knowledge that is claimed modulates very quickly into the claim that nature "can so inform / The mind that is within us" (125–126) that our cheerful faith in life is undisturbed. That this can or might be so is no guarantee that it will be so. Just what potentiality for informing our lives so as to produce cheerfulness is in fact actualized? When and how does this actualization of this potentiality take place? Exactly by what, when, and how might "all / The dreary intercourse of daily life" (130–131) be transformed? These questions have no answers, at least not within this poet's movements of consciousness. Hence "Our cheerful faith, that all which we behold / Is full of blessings" (133–134) remains a faith, perhaps all too vainly willed, rather than an article of knowledge.

(7) "Therefore let . . . / Thy memory be as a dwelling place" (134, 141) [lines 134–146]. The "therefore let . . . " of line 134 explicitly begins the prayer announced in line 121 ("this prayer I make"). It asks for Dorothy both now to persist in her naturalness or natural connection to nature and "in after years" (137) for her memory to be "as a dwelling-place / For all sweet sounds and harmonies" (141–142). The prayer is that she should at least preserve in her maturer consciousness a sense of past connection to nature and its beneficent influences. Yet this prayer for Dorothy quickly modulates for the poet into thoughts about himself. In a question to himself that is not marked as a question but rather as a declarative interjection within his own consciousness, Wordsworth asks "with what healing thoughts / Of tender joy wilt thou then remember me, / And these my exhortations" (144–146). The anxieties and doubts that haunt him are made explicit in this interrogative movement of his own consciousness. Will Dorothy, or anyone else for that matter, remember him, and if so, how ("with what healing thoughts") and why? What have his life in time and his just now occurring course of experience and reflection meant? Has he been a subject who has lived, fully and memorably, or not? No doctrine is available to ground any certainty of the achievement of the life of a subject. Only exhortations are possible; no declarations and no proofs can either ground the significance of a life or control the responses of any audience, even an audience as intimately present as Dorothy is in the scene. Prayer, not declaration, is the appropriate mode of acknowledgment of the ungroundedness of any claims to fullness of value on behalf of a human life in time.

(8) "Nor, perchance . . . wilt thou then forget" (146, 149) [lines 146–159]. Within the concluding prayer, the topic of death, and so of the significance of a life that is bounded by death, is raised explicitly.

"Nor, perchance— / If I should be where I no more can hear thy voice" (146–148) implies, given Dorothy's role as instance of a saving audience in general, "if I should be where no saving voice, no answering glance, neither Dorothy's nor anyone else's, is to be found." Within the awareness of death and the finite subjectivity bounded by it, one can declare very little, can say only "nor perchance wilt thou then forget," not "you will not forget." And yet a standing together, here and now, is possible, and that this standing together may be remembered is, at least here and now, enough to afford the poet some sense of stability and continuing selfhood. It is possible that the feeling or attitude borne by a subject so standing in this spot, the feeling or attitude of "deeper zeal" (154), may be appropriate to the life of a subject as such in this spot, and so it too may stand in another's memory. The poet confesses feelings ("deeper zeal" [154], "to me . . . dear" [158–159]) and claims aptness and exemplarity both for them and for his confession of them. This claim and confession cannot be grounded in any argument. Perhaps either the feeling or the confession of feeling has been vainly constructed. Yet they may stand. Time will tell.

IV

"Each individual that comes into the world is a new beginning; the universe itself is, as it were, taking a fresh start in him and trying to do something, even if on a small scale, that it has never done before."[43] If John Dewey is right about this, then there is in the particularity of each person also a standing exteriority to the pure manifestation of the essence of human subjectivity in time and nature. Geoffrey Hartman has characterized Wordsworth as a poet as "a 'limitour,' licensed to haunt only the borders of the country from which imagination comes and to which it seeks to return."[44] The discursive subjectivity that is constructed through the work of the imagination in arriving at a point of view and that is bound up with apperceptive awareness and awareness of variously attentive others stands apart from the full, meaningful naturalness of subjectivity that it would wish to achieve by establishing an absolute, value-

and stance-affording connection to nature and culture as such. "The terror of discontinuity or separation enters . . . as soon as the imagination truly enters."[45] As a result, Wordsworth's effort to find in nature a fully saving genius loci or natural source of transcendent meaningfulness founders. He can only wander from one moment to another of what is felt, almost, to be an accession to meaningfulness, but an accession that remains internally fragmented. Wordsworth's "quest to localize his Idea of [A Saving] Nature in Nature fails."[46] And so the pursuit of such moments goes on. Apart from such moments, there is the conventionalized, less meaningful life of ordinary subjectivity, caught up in circuits of antagonism ("evil tongues, / Rash judgments, [and] the sneers of selfish men, / [And] greetings where no kindness is" [128–130]), a life that motivates, always, a wish for a fuller, more meaningful life of an exemplary, stabilized subject as such. The voice that arises out of the moments of almost accession to meaningfulness, almost achievement of exemplarity, "is the voice of a man who has been separated from the hope he affirms."[47] Hartman has characterized the progress of *The Prelude* as "no argument, but a vacillation between doubt and faith,"[48] and this halted progress is evident, too, in the waverings of prayerful hope and recurrent uncertainty in "Tintern Abbey." Wordsworth's "curious and never fully clarified restlessness" is, Hartman suggests, "the ultimate confession of his poetry."[49]

Though they afford no doctrine to guide us, perhaps such vacillations and confessions show us something (though only something) of the lives of human subjects as such. Wordsworth's expression of his internalized quest romance, showing arrival at a fuller assurance crossed with doubt, enacts a romance of subject and world that is both strongly subjectivized and aimed at increased life in the world. If the modality of aiming is that of reflection, rehearsal, and conjecture more than specific, actual worldly political praxis, that is perhaps in part because the world of England in 1798 does not yet readily admit specific, sustained practices of wholeheartedness in daily life. Hence Wordsworth's poetry of reflection, rehearsal, and conjecture functions in relation to that world as disturbance, provocation, and placeholder, not only or simply as a source of reassurance. Our world may differ from Wordsworth's politically, culturally, cognitively, and technologically in manifold ways, but it stands no less in need of the kind of reassurance mixed with disturbance that Wordsworth's poetry affords. Promises of things not seen that remain unfulfilled arise within the lives of discursive human subjects, and they function, sometimes, critically and productively in relation to those lives, for those who have ears to hear.

5

The Ends of Literary Narrative

Rilke's "Archaic Torso of Apollo"

The claim of works of literature to represent truths about the world is, at best, peculiar. Most literary works are fictional. Authors spend their time and energies in thematizing, in developing attitudes toward subject matters, and in seeking formal power and coherence. There are no procedures in view that can arrive at results about matters independent of human subjects and attitudes. In contrast, a proof in mathematics ends by reaching its final line, where each line that is not an axiom is generated in explicit accord with a rule of inference that in principle anyone might follow. Reports of experimental results generated in a lab specify procedures that were followed in setting up equipment and carrying out tests. While they often also offer conjectural interpretations of results and suggestions for further work, they describe minimally a procedure that anyone might follow in order to achieve a like-enough result. Hence we can speak readily of objective evidence that a certain state of affairs can be produced thus and so. In statistical social science, one finds reports of results from questionnaires or other data about populations expressed in numerical terms. Under the assumption that a larger population will not be too different from a sample, one can draw conclusions about distributions of traits and tendencies of development. History undertakes to tell us what happened, and the claims of professional historians are supported with reference to primary sources, indicated in footnotes. In economics, one often finds abstract mathematical models that describe processes of income distribution or GNP growth, for example, that are supposed to occur underneath a confusing surface of extra variables that induce deviations from the model. Among these cognitive practices, literature is perhaps most like economics in giving a model of certain processes in the world. This is scant comfort, however, since whether the processes described by economic models really do occur, on the one hand, or are rather fairy tales invented by clever calculators, on the other, is itself a subject of more than a little dispute. Literary models, moreover, if that is what literary texts offer us, are in even worse shape, since they focus only on very small numbers of mostly made-up cases, and they lack even the potential of refinement through the incorporation of further data.

Instead of focusing on literature as a form of cognitive work, then, we might think of works of literature as aiming at producing a certain sort of pleasure. If we further suppose that all pleasures are subjective and rankable only in terms of duration and intensity, then the point of literary works would be exhausted in their consumption, and there is not much more to be said than this. As Bentham notoriously remarked, all other things being equal, pushpin is as good as poetry.

This view is unsatisfying, however, in that the experience of reading a powerful literary work is not really much like the experience of eating an ice cream cone or wallowing in a warm bath. It takes some work to pay attention. It is not exactly fun at every instant. The pleasure, if that is the right word, seems not to have much to do with sensory processes but more with the work that the reader is doing. And surely writers are trying to do something that is both cognitively available to their audiences and cognitively significant. But then, again, works of literature do not offer us results that are much like those of mathematics, laboratory science, history, or statistical social science. So we are faced with a puzzle. We seem to learn something from reading literature, but we have trouble explaining exactly how or what we learn—at least when we are in the grip of a certain picture of knowledge as the methodologically correct achievement of a fact-stating result.

It is easy to suggest that there must be a third way—between the forms of knowledge that are available in other disciplines and mere, predominantly sensible pleasure—in which literature is significant. We can see that this suggestion makes sense when we contrast art in general with scientific knowledge, on the one hand, and decoration and entertainment, on the other. Art is somehow in the middle here. If we are offered too many "flat" facts by a particular work, we are likely to find it merely journalistic and to want more pleasure. If we are offered too much pleasure, we are likely to find the work either decorative or an escapist guilty pleasure, like the novels of Ian Fleming or Dan Brown, say. We want, at least sometimes, to work harder and to learn more than that. But just how can we do this? The mere postulation of a third way does not yet answer this question.

In their valuable comprehensive survey *Truth, Fiction, and Literature*, Peter Lamarque and Stein Haugom Olsen explore a number of ways of thinking about literature as a source of knowledge. Centrally, they consider the following three suggestions: (1) Literary works might help us to know "what it is like" to be (or to be in the situation of) a certain character, in the sense of "subjective knowledge" characterized by Thomas Nagel and worked out with regard to literature by Dorothy Walsh. Against this, Lamarque and Olsen object first that while we have experiences while reading, we mostly have our own experiences, not the experiences of Leda or Leopold Bloom, Yeats or Joyce. In particular, we mostly observe or imagine characters having experiences. And while we take an interest in this observation, we are not learning the felt qualia of, say, fried kidney for Leopold Bloom. Second, even if we did get some sense of what things are like for characters from reading literary fiction, it is strained, Lamarque and Olsen suggest, to describe what we get as learning something. There are no methods in view for accrediting or testing any knowledge claims, such as there are in the sciences, and much of what we might think we learn we must in fact already have known in order to understand what is going on: for example, that rape is a violent, terrifying, and world-altering experience.[1] Or (2) literary works might enable us to enrich our store of concepts, or they might modify our sense of the application conditions of concepts we already possess, as Catherine Wilson and D. Z. Phillips have suggested. Against this suggestion, Lamarque and Olsen object that while some literary works might help us to deploy new concepts or to refigure the conditions of their application, this is by no means necessary for a work to have literary value. Second, and more sharply, they suggest that some authors sometimes explore the same concepts and conditions of application in different works, so that when one reads a second work, for example, a later play by Ibsen, one may not learn anything new. But the later work nonetheless has literary value; hence learning about concepts and their application conditions is not necessary for literary value (378–386). Or (3) it might be that literary works help us to become better perceivers of the moral lives of persons and so better reasoners about what it is good or right to do when, as Martha Nussbaum and Hilary Putnam have suggested. Against this suggestion, Lamarque and Olsen object first that improvement in moral reasoning is by no means brought about by all successful literary works, and, second, that having or furthering the correct valuational stance is not a necessary condition for literary value: we can and do value as successful works with whose stances and points of view we disagree (386–394).

One might suspect that there is something wrong here with Lamarque and Olsen's "divide and dismiss" strategy. Perhaps what we get from reading literature is some mixture of subjective knowledge, improvement of our conceptual capacities, and moral insight. Lamarque and Olsen themselves offer the positive suggestion that literature "develops themes that are only vaguely felt or formulated in daily life and gives them a 'local habitation and a name'" (452).[2] "Giving a name" at least hints that some sort of cognitive achievement is on offer. Literary appreciation, they further remark, "constitutes its own form of insight, its own kind of interpretation of thematic concepts" (409). But this form of insight, they argue, is better construed as the cultivation of *understanding* than as the acquisition of knowledge of true propositions. "Literary works can contribute to the development and understanding of the deepest, most revered of a culture's conceptions without advancing propositions, statements, or hypotheses about them" (22). "We can imagine, ponder, entertain thoughts, or speculate about something without any commitment to the truth of our ruminations" (11). Literary practice is best understood as an imaginative exploration of themes that is guided by the literary work, which undertakes "to develop in depth, through subject and form, a theme which is in some sense central to human concerns" (450).

But while this talk of understanding is a good start, it leaves us not so far beyond where we were before. Exactly what do we understand when we understand the theme of a literary work? How is this understanding related to, but different from, propositional knowledge either that the world is thus and so or that the author thought thus and so (itself just another fact about the world)? How is this understanding cultivated by the experience of the work itself? What does it mean to "develop a theme *in depth*"? What, if anything, makes such development valuable in human life?

John Gibson suggests that the important cognitive work of literature consists in "bringing into full view our standards of representation [and] our linguistic criteria for what the world is."[3] A literary work may show some phenomenon "just as it is" (61); for example, we may see the essence of racism in the figure of Iago (61–62). Shakespeare's presentation of Iago "draws together at . . . a level of clarity and order everything we call racism" (63), thus making the shape of our concept available to us for acknowledgment. This suggestion too is a useful start. But what it fails so far to explain is how we can fail to know the criteria of some of our concepts and, hence, why we need to explore and acknowledge them. Surely we need already to have some pretty clear command of the concept of racism in order to understand Iago's actions at all. What further dimensions of our concept, then, are subject to repression or forgetting, and how do the details of the presentation of Iago as a literary character activate these dimensions? What, exactly, is the cognitive import of having our concepts activated and somehow "filled in"?[4]

Gibson further suggests that a general reason why we turn to works of literature is that we are able there to "read the story of our shared form of life" (50). This is the suggestion we must pursue if we are to have any hope of unpacking the jointly cognitive and emotional work of acknowledging and working through that reading literature makes available to us. So what is the story of our form of life? This enormous question is one that will have to be faced if we are to make any progress here.

Part of that story is the playing out of a biologically engendered imperative to survive. We need to eat, sleep, protect ourselves, and procreate in order to survive as a species, and we are, so far, wired well enough for success in these endeavors. In the absence of extraordinary strength or speed, we have managed cope with our environments mostly through superior cunning. We are better at recognizing and manipulating more features of our environments than are members of other species. In particular, as concept-mongering creatures, we are able not only to see objects brutely, as it were, as members of kinds; we are also able to see them from a point of view, as this or that. For example, a stone may be recognized by us as a weapon, a piece of building material, or an implement for scratching or shaping. A fundamental part of learning language is developing this repertoire of seeing an object as something. We manage this achievement not simply through picking up on the individuals-just-sorted-into-natural-kinds that are present in our environment. Other animals do this as well, but they lack our conceptual repertoire. My dog responds to the sounds of squirrels but does not think of them as mammals or rodents or nut gatherers. We, however, manage feats like this by picking up not only on our environments brutely, but also by picking up on how other human subjects are interacting with our shared environment, by picking up on their points of view on things.[5] Our having of a wide repertoire of concepts and application criteria, enabling manifold different responses to our environment, is not a matter only of matching inner idea or Platonic archetype or brain state with object. It is a matter of learning to see things within multiple and shifting contexts of engagement and use, a matter of catching on to a large number of things that are done or might be done, by others and by oneself, at once with objects and with words, within practical engagements. In coming to be masters of words that encode objects and events seen in one way or another, in relation to multiple contexts of engagement and possible response, we are neither machines nor the quasi-automatons of Wittgenstein's language game (2) in *Philosophical Investigations*. Rather we are creatures who have become capable of a life of plastic attention—capable, that is, of culture.

The fact that we develop conceptual consciousness not only in relation to problems of biological survival but also in relation to cultural contexts of flexible attention and engagement brings with it certain distinctive burdens and possibilities. Not only is one trying to survive; one is also trying to play the game of attending according to concepts both with others and in competition with others to have one's own point of view and way of playing the game recognized. Concepts and words, for all that they register features of our environments there to be registered, are also, in their lives within cultural contexts of shifting attention and engagement, both stable enough to permit communication and sharing of a point of view on things and tolerant of new uses as new contexts of attention and interest develop.[6] Hence coming to language and conceptual consciousness brings with it uncertainties about how to go on from where we are or where one is. Am I playing the game in the right way? Is my conceptual performance such that it can and should be taken up by others? Do I really know what I'm doing?[7] What are evident and exemplary fluency and command in making moves with words? Just who do I think I am, and am I right about that?

These questions are such that they cannot and do not arise at every moment; comprehensive skepticism is not a genuinely available stance in life. But they are also such that they can always arise at some point, at least in modernity, where manifestly different ways of life develop and make themselves present in awareness. As the Kantian tradition emphasizes, a life with concepts is a life in which questions of judgment are always potentially in view, and the fact of continuing responsibility in and for conceptual performance is unavoidable. (It would be a mistake to see our concepts as self-standing representational "entities" existing outside of circuits of mimesis and training.) R. G. Collingwood tells the following wonderful story about what it is like to come to conceptual consciousness and language, thus becoming a subject of and in culture:

> A child throws its bonnet off its head and into the road with the exclamation "Hattiaw." By comparison with the self-conscious cry discussed earlier in the present section, this represents a highly developed and sophisticated use of language. To begin with, consider the emotion involved. The child might remove its bonnet because it felt physically uncomfortable in it, hot or tickled or the like; but the satisfaction expressed by the cry of "Hattiaw" is not a merely psycho-physical pleasure like that of rubbing a fly off the nose. What is expressed is a sense of triumph, an emotion arising out of the possession of self-consciousness. The child is proving itself as good a man as its mother, who has previously taken its bonnet off with the words it is now imitating; better than its mother, because now she has put the bonnet on and wants it to stay on, so there is a conflict of wills in which the child feels himself victor.[8]

As this example shows, even very early on in our life as possessors of conceptual consciousness and self-consciousness, we bear distinctive emotions and attitudes toward our situations. We are capable of accepting, working through, and expressing these emotions, with a resulting sense of a certain kind of triumph, when our point of view is recognized by others through our performances. We are capable also of sullenly shirking our emotions, avoiding them, or otherwise failing to express them, with a consequent sense of disappointment, frustration, and failure, and, sometimes, with a further wish to escape or reject the burdens of the responsibility for expression. When this happens, we then suffer or merely undergo our emotions, as we remain stuck in the state of having what Spinoza calls an inadequate idea of an affection: we don't know what is worth caring about; we take no delight in the investment of our energies in our performances, and confused, unexpressed feelings wash over us.[9] Our actions are as much reactions as expressions of our selfhood. Philosophical skepticism and its intimate antagonist epistemological realism are both at bottom misbegotten intellectualized efforts to repudiate the situation and expressive possibilities of conceptual consciousness and self-consciousness by describing them away. (What Stanley Cavell calls the truth of skepticism is the fact that the skeptic, at least, registers a certain failure and disappointment that attach to these efforts.)[10] More happily, however, there are also what Charles Altieri calls "the kinds of satisfactions that are available for agents simply because of the qualities of consciousness they bring to what they are feeling."[11] We can do something with these qualities of consciousness. As Wordsworth argues in the "Preface to *Lyrical Ballads*," the poet, through thinking "long and deeply" in relation to our feelings, may uncover "what is really important to men," with the result that, when this course of discovery is taken up and followed, "the understanding of the Reader must necessarily be in some degree enlightened, and his affections strengthened and purified."[12] Friedrich Hölderlin on infinite satisfaction[13] and John Dewey on consummatory experience[14] describe in quite similar terms the distinctive sorts of satisfactions open to us as human subjects. The achievement of further understanding coupled with strengthened and purified affections, with both understanding and affections then discharged in a dense, medium-specific performance of working through, in which a point of view is made manifest and recognition and like-mindedness are successfully solicited, is what I have elsewhere called the achievement of expressive freedom.[15] It has, I think, some claim to be regarded as an immanent telos of human life, made both possible, partially, and valuable for us by our mysterious possession of conceptual consciousness and self-consciousness, developed and worked out in relation to public media of expression.

It is impossible to prove the correctness of this view according to the standards of proof that are held in place in the Cartesian tradition. (Those standards were specifically developed in order to block talk of the purposes of things.) But it remains nonetheless an articulation of what is going on in human life that may be unavoidable and illuminating. If it has any chance of being right, then Lamarque and Olsen are wrong when they remark that "mostly, we simply do not meet the grand themes in trivial daily life" (455). Yes and no. Yes, we do not meet them clearly formulated and perspicuously manifested there; there is too much muddle for that, and there are too many different circumstances in which lives are led for it to be just obvious that we are in pursuit of expressive freedom. But no, we do meet these themes there latently, to be acknowledged, as we come to see our lives as in part caught up in situ in the pursuit of expressive freedom, involving articulate clarity and wholeheartedness of interest in life.

Great writers, then, manage to achieve expressiveness: that is, to face up to and work through the emotions and attitudes that come with being a human subject, as those emotions and attitudes are given specific contours in specific situations. They make it manifest for themselves and for us how a specifically shaped emotion, mood, or feeling has been brought about in or by a situation and how, further, that emotion, mood, or feeling can be accepted as appropriate. As a result, the emotion, mood, or feeling is actively accepted, not passively suffered. Barbara Herrnstein Smith describes the achievement of poetic closure from the reader's point of view in just these terms:

Closure occurs when the concluding portion of a poem creates in the reader a sense of appropriate cessation. It announces and justifies the absence of further development; it reinforces the feeling of finality, completion, and composure which we value in all works of art; and it gives ultimate unity and coherence to the reader's experience of the poem, by providing a point from which all the preceding elements may be received comprehensively and their relations grasped as part of a significant design.[16]

For the reader, that is to say, the poem itself is experienced as coherent, closed, and designed, as its parts form a self-completing whole. This experience is a function of form, but not of form alone. It occurs in part because the poet has succeeded in making sense of experience and emotion, has succeeded in working them through to achieve acceptance and composure. As Herrnstein Smith notes, "the experience of closure is the complex product of both formal and thematic elements" (40). This means that the poet has found, formally, words and structures to thematize, connect, and accept experiences and emotions that were initially burdensome, troubling, exhilarating, or provocative. She goes on to note that many contemporary poems, beginning with Eliot and reaching a high point in Robert Lowell, exhibit increasingly "dialectical-associative" thematic structure. "In much modern poetry," she remarks, "the occasion for a poem is . . . likely to be the existence of an ultimately unresolvable process" (247). There is what she calls a "poetry of non-statement" (254) that takes both subjective-lyrical stream-of-consciousness guises and objectivist-imagist-language play guises. The reason for this development is that we have grown, appropriately, skeptical of the availability and livability of "they lived happily ever after." Nineteenth-century novels, as both Henry James and David Lodge have mordantly remarked, seem to end only with marriage, death, or an inheritance. In contrast, we have grown suspicious of the availability and value of these kinds of closure in life, which seems to us to be more complicated than that. But even in the contemporary poetry of antistatement, the shape and feeling of a particular instance of perplexity are expressively worked through, at least when things go well. The writer and the reader afterward come to know and accept exactly how there are complexities of situation and feeling. As Herrnstein Smith puts it, "a poem allows us to know what we know, including our illusions and desires, by giving us the language in which to acknowledge it" (154). Such an achievement of acknowledgment is available and important for us just insofar as we are human subjects who attempt to lead lives actively, with senses of meaning and of appropriate responsiveness to events, unlike Nietzsche's cows, who do little besides undergo their lives.[17] Unlike other animals, we remember and anticipate incidents quite widely, together with an awareness of how incidents and things are seen by others from multiple points of view. And so we wonder: Who am I to see, remember, and anticipate things like this? To what extent are my point of view and emotions toward things apt and appropriate? Am I genuinely acting as a reasonable subject in seeing things and feeling as I do?

In the grip of a healthy empiricism, it is of course possible to find this talk of expressive freedom and of leading a life actively to be quite misplaced in relation to what is after all also a sheerly material situation. There is, again, nothing like a proof by Cartesian standards that expressive freedom is the immanent telos of human life. But what does it look like, according to this conception, when someone rejects it and denies that expressive freedom matters for us and that it is partially, but only partially, available to us through different actions in different settings? (It is possible to say anything.) The Humean-skeptical, Darwininan-naturalist insistence that we are nothing but natural beings who must simply cope with things and the Cartesian-Platonist insistence that absolute knowledge of our place in nature can guide us if we but somehow think aright both appear as hysteria-driven denials of what it is to be a finite, active being in time. "You ask me," Nietzsche once wrote, "which of the philosophers' traits are really idiosyncrasies? For example, their lack of historical sense, their hatred of the very idea of becoming, their Egypticism. They think that they show their *respect* for a subject when they de-historicize it, *sub specie aeterni*—when they turn it into a mummy."[18] To deny that our lives are caught up in becoming and in possibilities of the achievement of expressive freedom in part, but only in part, in relation to it can look like an attempt to deny or kill human life because it is too painful.

Yet as Nietzsche also remarked, it can also sometimes happen—if and when we manage ourselves to work through and express our emotions in a dense, commanding performance, or if and when as readers if we follow and participate in the workings-through of others—that we are left with the sense, at least for a time, "that life is at the bottom of things, despite all the changes of appearances, indestructibly powerful and pleasurable."[19] In a late notebook entry,

Nietzsche describes the authentic state, a state that may either occur in life or be "set up" in art, as the state

> in which we put a *transfiguration and plenitude* into things and work at shaping them until they reflect back to us our own plenitude and lust for life. . . . Art reminds us of states of animal vigour; it's on the one hand a surplus and overflow of flourishing corporeality into the world of images and wishes; on the other a rousing of the animal function through images and wishes of intensified life—a heightening of the feeling of life, stimulus for it.[20]

Within experience, a pattern can sometimes be discerned, partially and dimly, in our relations as subjects to things and events, and emotions, feelings, attitudes, and moods can be experienced and worked through as appropriate to that pattern. Discovery and exhilaration are mixed with a sense also of mystery and complexity in the face of a becoming, a life in time, that is not wholly masterable. For this reason, great endings, as Steven Winn remarks, "define and disappoint, frustrate and gratify. They confer meaning and confirm the structure of what's come before—in a movie, a sonata, a work of fiction. But they also kill off pleasure, snap us out of the dream, and clamp down order on experience that we, as citizens of the modern world, believe to be open-ended, ambiguous, and unresolved."[21]

This experience of an ending is like what Aristotle describes as the catharsis—at once the clarification and unburdening—of an emotion in relation to a situation. But, as Frank Kermode notes, whereas "for Aristotle the literary plot was analogous to the plot of the world in that both were eductions from the potency of matter,"[22] which eductions are presided over purposively by divine intelligence, for us the sense of plot in life proceeds at least in part from our own "store of contrivances" (40), as we are driven by "a need to live by [a] pattern" (109). We half believe in these patterns, as we experience our lives within them and experience possibilities of clarification of our situation. And yet we remain also aware of our own role as contrivers, aware of the lack of a presiding pattern that is everywhere evident in human life and aware also of our own failures to live in perfect freedom and infinite satisfaction, in the face of the mysterious complexities of becoming. And so we tell stories and attempt to work through our emotions in relation to the particulars of changing situations, so that we can, as Kermode puts it, both "avoid the regress into [a] myth" of presiding purposiveness and yet preserve the sense that "the scene [of human significance] has not yet been finally and totally struck" (43). Fictions that find plots, so as to work through emotions in relation to situations and experiences, remain for us both "deeply distrusted," since they are only our contrivances, and "humanly indispensable," since only these contrivances can give us the sense of leading a life meaningfully and actively. They offer us a way, even the way, to cope with both anxiety at a sense of the pervasive contingency of things and bad faith in fixed, master supernatural plots we can no longer trust (151). They are our means of coping with "the tension or dissonance between paradigmatic form and contingent reality" (133), between the sense that every life is a parable of each, with meaning to be found, and the sense that there are only material happenstance and subjective "preference having."

That we may through producing and effectively receiving exemplary works of art come to a fuller, more animated, more ensouled life, beyond mere preference having, yet also as individuals free from submission to alien authority, is a major subject of Rainer Maria Rilke's *Neue Gedichte* (*New Poems*, 1907; second part, 1908). The new poems in general and the Thing-poems in particular result significantly from Rilke's responses to the French sculptor Auguste Rodin. Rilke worked as Rodin's secretary in 1905 and 1906, he wrote a 1903 monograph and a 1907 lecture on Rodin, and the first volume of *Neue Gedichte* is dedicated to him.[23] Rodin's influence is evident in the *Neue Gedichte* in two distinct ways. His sculptures provided for Rilke a model of an animated, all but living work of art. As Judith Ryan puts it, "In Rodin's sculpture, the interplay of light between the various surfaces creates for Rilke the sense of something that continues to shape itself before the eye of the beholder,"[24] as though the sculpture were alive. Second, "Rodin's ideal of persistent workmanship,"[25] his sense of the importance of patience and craft, makes itself felt in the tightly controlled formal structure of the poems. The effect of animation in the poems then arises from the way in which inspiration and living energy, ideals Rilke associated with Theodore de Banville,[26] are submitted to formal control, in order to construct a living whole.

In a famous sonnet appearing as the first poem of *New Poems: Second Part*, Rilke describes what it is like to come suddenly, from within one's middle situation, between dead, foreign materiality and perfect transcendence, to a sense of possibilities of fuller animation.

ARCHAÏSCHER TORSO APOLLOS

Wir kannten nicht sein unerhörtes Haupt,
darin die Augenäpfel reiften. Aber
sein Torso glüht noch wie ein Kandelaber,
in dem sein Schauen, nur zurückgeschraubt,

sich hält und glänzt. Sonst könnte nicht der Bug
der Brust dich blenden, und im leisen Drehen
der Lenden könnte nicht ein Lächeln gehen
zu jener Mitte, die die Zeugung trug.

Sonst stünde dieser Stein entstellt und kurz
unter der Schultern durchsichtigem Sturz
und flimmerte nicht so wie Raubtierfelle;

und brächte nicht aus allen seinen Rändern
aus wie ein Stern: denn da ist keine Stelle,
die dich nicht sieht. Du mußt dein Leben ändern.

ARCHAIC TORSO OF APOLLO

We cannot know his legendary head
with eyes like ripening fruit. And yet his torso
is still suffused with brilliance from inside,
like a lamp, in which his gaze, now turned to low,

gleams in all its power. Otherwise
the curved breast could not dazzle you so, nor could
a smile run through the placid hips and thighs
to that dark center where procreation flared.

Otherwise this stone would seem defaced
beneath the translucent cascade of the shoulders
and would not glisten like a wild beast's fur:

would not, from all the borders of itself,
burst like a star: for here there is no place
that does not see you. You must change your life.[27]

This poem describes not simply an object but preeminently an experience of an object, an experience had by or available to a "we." The poem embodies an effort to formulate and to work through an experience of perplexity, both for the speaker and for other subject-viewers, to whom and for whom the poet may speak. The statue fragment is characterized above all in terms of its effect on the speaker-viewer, in its overwhelming presence to a viewing consciousness. Within that experience, the fragment presents itself as having an inside, felt as a source of expressive and sexual power that is brought to fullness of presence in its outer surface. The formed surface glows (*glüht*), gleams (*glänzt*), blinds the viewer (*dich blenden*), and bears a smile (*ein Lächeln*) as a promise of responsive sexuality. Its parts are not detached or misplaced (*entstellt*); instead the stone glistens (*flimmerte*) in its translucent falling (*durchsichtigem Sturz*), as though everywhere breaking out of its borders (*brächte aus allen seinen Rändern*), as if seeing us from every part of itself. These verbs describe the presence of what is inner in what is outer, in a way that is typical in Rilke's mature work. As Ryan puts it, "the exploration of the relation between inner and outer realities, an attempt to transfigure loss, and an understanding of the aesthetic as a phenomenon of displacement are all characteristic features . . . of Rilke's later writing."[28] The speaker's gaze moves from (absent) head down the front of the torso, following the arc of the glowing surface from prowlike breast to curving loins to genitals. The image of a smile in the turn of the loins is drawn, Ryan notes, "from an essay by Mallarmé on Théodore de Banville, whom Mallarmé regards as the supreme lyric poet of his time."[29] The image of the turned-back (*zurückgeschraubt*, as in a gas jet turned back from flickering in order to provide steady illumination) candelabra is, Ryan suggests, "a recollection of Mallarmé's sonnet 'Le Tombeau de Charles Baudelaire.'"[30] Together, these two images emphasize the presence of controlled, animating, procreative power showing itself in the statue's surface. The statue fragment is intensely expressively present, so that it serves as a standing rebuke to us, who fail to bring our own personality, intelligence, and expressive and sexual powers to full embodied expression but instead live at second hand, palely under conventions that lack full life for us. Hence the fragment rebukes us for failing to be what we dimly feel we might be and ought to be as possessors of unexpressed inner intelligence and power: more fully animate, more fitly ensouled.

And yet the poem is itself a classical sonnet, with an octave rhyming abba cddc followed by a sestet rhyming eef gfg. In place of a classical turn or volta after the octave, however, there are two turns: in line 5, with a move into the subjunctive in order to clarify and deepen the initial sense of the fragment's glowing, and then in line 14, with the sudden and brutal ascription of quasi-agentive sight to the fragment, issuing in a rebuke to the viewer-subject, who falls under its gaze and judgment. This rebuke, felt by the viewer-subject and addressed first to himself and thence to us, his readers, is startling. But the eef gfg scheme of the sestet houses this rebuke in a structure of strong formal coherence, giving a sense of appropriateness and closure to the experience. Through the tightly controlled form and images, the rebuke is earned by the experience as it is registered in the poem itself. The poem itself, that is to say, strikes us, through its form and images, as a composed, animated, ensouled whole. As Ryan notes, in the first poem, "Early Apollo," of *New Poems: First Part*, Rilke himself equates the overwhelming effect of an Apollo statue with the overwhelming effect of poetry in general. "There is nothing in the head, the speaker says, '*was verhindern könnte, daß der Glanz aller Gedichte uns fast tödlich träfe*' (which could prevent us from being almost fatally wounded by the radiance of the poems)."[31] The poem both rebukes us, its readers, in the way that the fragment has rebuked the viewer-subject, and shows us concretely that the housing of expressive power in controlled surface is still possible and commanding for us, even after the loss of the older dispensations.

For the poet, and for us who follow and share in the poet's experience, first of the fragment and then of the poem itself as constructed yet as it were living object, it thus remains possible for experience to mean something, possible to have an adequate idea of an affection, with full investment in one's responses to things, at least in principle. The trouble is that we are mostly too half-hearted to take this possibility seriously, perhaps half-hearted because the late modern world is so thoroughgoingly complex and opaque. Forms of technological and social expertise multiply and diverge, so that it becomes harder to sustain a sense of how they do or might form a meaningful whole. They seem detached or misplaced (*entstellt*), and coping and compromise seem inevitably to displace the pursuit of wholeheartedness. It may be a part of wisdom simply to accept much of this, much of the time. And yet: formal coherence blended with original power is possible and compelling. This poem exists, and its force can be felt, perhaps at some time by many and often by some: you must change your life.

To be sure, this poem is in a way a fiction. It does not report a material reality that is independent of subjectivity and discerned through practices of measurement. Rather it tells a story about an experience and its significance, where the terms of significance involve a sense of emplotment and possibility in human life that are not simply given in tradition or simple sense experience. That sense of emplotment and possibility is itself felt, both by the poet initially and subsequently by us who follow the poet's feeling and thinking, as shaped or contrived in human time, just as first the fragment and then the poem have been shaped or contrived: we, like the poet, must construct it. Yet this sense is also felt as inevitable, present, and altogether other than arbitrarily invented: it is commanded of us in our contrivings by something that makes itself manifest in the formal and thematic working through of experience. In this working through, both the emplotment of this experience and the relation of this particular emplotment to a larger emplotment of human life are both constructed and accepted as given, by the poet and by us. This half-constructed, half-given experience of emplotment does not, however, admit of being fully unpacked and generalized into a master plot of human life as such. Perhaps either the unanticipatedly other and new will inevitably disrupt any settled life policy; perhaps nature and passion are the always present unruly birthplaces of any civil order. No recipe for how one is to change one's life so as to achieve expressive power is on offer. Instead the speaker (by the statue) and we (first by the statue, insofar as we share the we-position of the speaker, and then by the poem) are stopped and reminded that something better, we know not what, at least not in specific detail, haunts and draws us. The initial we-position of the speaker is both reinforced, insofar as anyone may take the statue and the poem as admonishment and provocation, and suspended, as the force of any injunction is felt by an individual viewer or reader bereft of any directions about how to follow it objectively and with others. A "we" is posed but also suspended as expressive intensity is urged on us as individuals, and modern life remains a scene of both banality and unparameterized possibility.

Perhaps we should not call what we get from deeply absorbing, cathartic, yet contingency-acknowledging workings through of experience knowledge. Even framing the issue about the role of literature in our lives in terms of knowledge as it is construed paradigmatically in the natural sciences expresses the theoretical philosopher's characteristic bad faith in wanting everything circumscribed and life guided by rationally obligatory rules. Yet we cannot live as human persons without this literature; what we get from it is a sense of life in a human reality that is, if marked by brute contingency, not everywhere dominated by it. Achievement of the free, powerful, and coherent ordering of the materials of one's life is possible—if not wholly and continuously, nonetheless occasionally and exemplarily. A form of life that needs a highly charged modernist reminder of this possibility is a form of life whose energies are in danger of flagging and whose preoccupations are less than fulfilling as they stand. A form of life that contains such reminders and contains readers capable of responding to them is a form of life in which hope remains alive as hope. Rilke may be taken to have known that his concluding injunction would be experienced as brutal, as difficult and all but unreceivable, and hence to have known that it is a wager that his writing can find or forge its audience. Against Rilke, perhaps it is right that, often, we should refuse the wager, as complexity, compromise, and common decency make cowards of us all. The brutalities of art's claims on us in the modern world should not be flattened into comfortable niceties. Yet it is not clear either that they always are or should be refused. The rest is silence: I cannot live to hear the news from England.

6.

"New Centers of Reflection Are Continually Forming"

Benjamin, Sebald, and Modern Human Life in Time

I

In a poignant passage in the introduction to his *Lectures on Fine Art* (1820), Hegel describes how, in his view, human subjects express themselves in the world through practical activity in order to recognize themselves.[1]

Man brings himself before himself by *practical* activity, since he has the impulse, in whatever is directly given to him, in what is present to him externally, to produce himself and therein equally to recognize himself. This aim he achieves by altering external things whereon he impresses the seal of his inner being and in which he now finds again his own characteristics. Man does this in order, as a free subject, to strip the external world of its inflexible foreignness and to enjoy in the shape of things only an external realization of himself. Even a child's first impulse involves this practical alteration of external things; a boy throws stones into a river and marvels at the circles drawn in the water as an effect in which he gains an intuition of something that is his own doing.[2]

Poignant though this passage is, one may nonetheless wonder at its claims. Is it the first impulse of human subjects, as subjects, to seek recognition of themselves and of the reasonableness of their doings in relation to external things? How dominant is this impulse in comparison with other impulses? (Many problems of survival, of coping with life, and of satisfying one's wants seem to have little on the face of it to do with seeking self-recognition.) Worse yet, how far is it genuinely possible to win self-recognition or to gain "an intuition of something that is [one's own] doing"? Perhaps such intuitions are only relatively fleeting in the face of the chaos and press of life, and perhaps they are available also only to the few who have "enough"—enough means, time, and training—and who live in good enough societies in which to carry out their efforts at self-expression and self-recognition. Perhaps there are other things that many people care about more fundamentally than they care about gaining a stable intuition of something that is one's own free and reasonable doing.

Hegel concedes that the life of Spirit, which includes at least the lives of human subjects in historical time, is marked by "tarrying with the negative" and by "death and devastation."[3] Establishing or expressing anything requires negation and its working through, always;[4] the life of Spirit is continually reforming itself in historical time. As Stephen Houlgate notes, "Hegel's philosophy . . . contains within itself a principle of aesthetic and religious *resistance* to its own 'totalizing claims.'"[5] Whatever their capacities for conceptually structured self-regulation and satisfaction within meaningful social roles, human beings remain also sensuous beings who stand in some need of feeling imaginatively that life makes (enough) sense. Moreover, as Terry Pinkard remarks, the shapes of our lives are not simply given, according to Hegel. Rather, "we *come to be* the kinds of agents we are," and so bear, at least potentially, at each moment "a 'negative' stance toward ourselves": we could become something we are, so far, not. This negative stance or open stance toward future possibility then "inflicts a kind of 'wound,' a *Zerissenheit*, a manner of being internally torn apart that demands healing,"[6] as we seek greater self-unity and more meaningful satisfaction. Or as Hegel himself puts it, "in the spiritual nature of man duality and inner conflict burgeon, and in their contradiction he is tossed about."[7]

And yet, according to Hegel, philosophy, together with the life of the Spirit—human life in time—with which it is interwoven, "proceeds to the cancellation"[8] of this opposition." Hegel argues that we are historically on the cusp of a time in which "*basically everyone*" will be able "to satisfy [his or her] knowledge and volition . . . within the actuality of the state,"[9] that is, within the framework of the modern democratic nation-state and its institutions of right. Basically all subjects will be able to see reflections of themselves in their doings, in ways that are simultaneously individual and yet stable and reasonable under modern institutions. Structural social revolution is and should be a thing of the past, and we may reasonably claim to live in large measure in reconciliation with actuality.[10]

After the horrors of the twentieth and twenty-first centuries, however, and with awareness of the persistence of problems of poverty and radical inequality, it scarcely requires much perceptiveness to wonder whether this is really possible. When one then considers further the insights of Marx and Althusser and of Nietzsche and Freud into social life and into standing pressures on individual psyches, then the prospects for a shared life of right—a community of reciprocal respect and recognition among free subjects who freely lead lives that are meaningful and reasonable under shared social institutions—seem dimmer yet. Even if a system of liberal civil rights is a relatively good idea for maintaining a degree of social peace and affording subjects a measure of liberty, no routes of direct political action promise to lead to a life of full freedom and right. Nor does theoretical-representational knowing as it is rigorously pursued in the experimental and mathematical sciences much point to solving problems of self-recognition and reciprocal recognition in worldly practice. We might then conclude that human subjects either do not or should not much care about the pursuit of recognition—the pursuit, that is, of stable senses, maintained by others and by themselves, of their own doings as individually chosen, free, reasonable, and satisfying. Yet that conclusion then makes it hard to see how human subjects engage in either self-cultivation or the cultivation of their social relations at all. These forms of cultivation—the sheer existences of cultures—do seem to embody the pursuit of some sort of expressive power, coherence, and means for the development and recognition of stable, reasonable, and satisfying identity. And yet such pursuits seem always to founder, perhaps inevitably to founder to some extent.

Walter Benjamin's writings on language, history, and culture offer us one way to think about how human beings live with the all but impossible task of the pursuit of recognition. Unlike Hegel, Benjamin begins from the thought that fullness of recognition—what would amount to a paradise of free and meaningful life on earth—is unavailable either on the basis of history as we have inherited it or through any particular specifiable efforts, political, cultural, or theoretical. In an essay written in 1916 but unpublished in his lifetime, Benjamin formulates the unavailability of utopia through or from present courses of culture by contrasting the fullness of the meaning of things to and for God with the standing failure to engage with things (and with each other) in fully meaningful ways that characterizes all human culture. He contrasts God's meaningful naming of things, bound up with understanding them in their proper places and interrelations, with what he calls the human overnaming of things, bound up with our taking them specifically this way or that, as objects of particular use, say, without living in full "resonance" with them. "Things have no proper names except in God. For in his creative word God called them into being, calling them by their proper names. In the language of men, however, they are overnamed. . . . The naming word in the knowledge of man must fall short of the creative word of God."[11] God, who made things freely and in accordance with fullness of understanding, knows and engages with things according to their proper natures and significances. The ways of knowing and engaging with things that is characteristic of human beings are contrasted with the way of God. No matter, then, what one thinks about the existence of God, the point must be that the ways of knowing and engaging with things that are characteristic of human beings are, all of them, one-sided and reflective of conflicts over what things are and how they are to be used. Culture—which is the embodiment of ways of conceiving of things and of making use of them—as it is made by human beings perpetuates one-sidedness and conflict rather than resolving them. Overnaming or living within particular mimetic circuits of conception and use is a form of overspecification that does not let things be in their full significance and prevents human beings from engaging with either materiality or with one another in ways that embody fullness of meaning. Overnaming is, therefore, "the deepest reason for all melancholy and (from the point of view of the thing) for all deliberate muteness. Overnaming as the linguistic being of melancholy points to another curious relation of language: the overprecision that obtains in the tragic relationship between the languages of human speakers."[12]

To say that relations between languages are tragic and characterized by overprecision is to say that some dimension of what is meant in a given language is somehow missed in its rendering in a second language, with tragic consequences. And that in turn must be because, to some extent, the ways of conceiving of and engaging with things opened up within a given language are not fully available for expression in a second language. All actual languages are marked by overprecise falling away from the fullness of meaning and attention embodied in the divine language. Given, further, that the boundaries of language identity may be as narrow as those of an individual speaker's idiolect, Benjamin's picture is of human subjects generally failing to some degree to understand how other human subjects "take" things and engage with them, hence failing to some degree to understand what other human subjects are doing, what might be reasonable and sensible.

This picture need by no means be taken as a Whorfian picture of subjects as somehow wholly sealed off from one another by boundaries of language and culture that are impermeable to translation. There is some good reason to think that some considerable success in translation and in understanding what others are up to is always possible in relation to any being whom we can recognize as a language-deploying and thinking subject at all.[13] But conflict nonetheless remains. There are standing practical difficulties among subjects in undertaking fully to understand how other subjects "take" things, what they are up to in engaging with them, and, so, what a free, meaningful, and reasonable life together under common "takings" might be like. There is, for us, no standpoint available outside the partiality that attaches to any point of view that any of us might occupy as finite subjects, no way to see things "whole" and untainted by overnaming within the always partly particularized mimetic circuits that one has inherited and developed. Practical problems of human relationship persist. That is the thought captured in Benjamin's contrast between God's calling things by their proper names and human overnaming.

Our ways of taking things conceptually and of engaging with them—no matter how widely shared, pragmatically useful, and historically sensible they may be—are not grounded on any grasp of ultimate, sempiternal reality. Something, some fullness of significance, is somehow missed in any way of taking and engaging with things (or with one another). And so, "within all linguistic formation [and within all repertoires of culture] a conflict is waged between what is expressed and expressible and what is inexpressible and unexpressed."[14] We are, always, failing to mean fully and transparently to others and to ourselves everything that might reasonably be meant in engaging with things and so failing also to live fully and transparently and meaningfully with others according to reason. Our languages and cultural practices ultimately express these facts, at least in certain moments in certain pockets of use. Experience is, therefore, not a matter only of simple classification of objects under concepts, without remainder, and it is not a matter of human subjects each fully knowing what they and each other are up to, according to articulated good reasons. Experience is rather a form of human life in which, sometimes, things happen unpredictably, coincidentally, and yet in such a way that unarticulated significances are displayed and felt. From within the repressed history of a language, something can make itself felt, and present overprecision can be disturbed. Such disturbances can also appear when one undertakes (but in some measure fails at) literary translation or through dislocations of one's ordinary habits of perception, as in travel.

Michael Rosen usefully characterizes Benjamin's understanding of experience as including a sense of the existence of "unseen affinities": relations among things or significances of things that are somehow missed within our ordinary articulations of what we are up to (within our ordinary "overnamings") but that nonetheless sometimes make themselves manifest. As Rosen puts it, "'unseen affinities' [such as the 'passion for roulette' in relation to 'the vogue for panoramas'], referring, as they do, to a subterranean level of awareness, are not such as, immediately and unambiguously, to strike the uninstructed observer; and yet it is their existence that provides Benjamin's concept of experience with its only possible verification."[15] There are, that is to say, within experience, ways of taking things and ways of engaging with things that seem to disrupt ordinary, articulated, planned ways of thinking, living, and working, and that in disrupting them seem to show exactly how specifically partial those ordinary ways are, just insofar as they are bound up with specific mimetic circuits of overnaming. Attention to these moments of surprise and disruption functions, then, not only as a verification of Benjamin's concept of experience as always partial and fallen but also as a reminder of our finitude and of what we have failed to achieve in the way of fullness of significance within the predominant parts of daily cultural life. Since such moments are always possible—since some surprises and disruptions always remain unrecuperated to transparent and reasonable social life, no matter how it develops—there can be no Hegelian recipe in the face of their permanent presence within life for achieving full human freedom in cultural life according to reason. For this reason, Benjamin characterizes his own method as that of evidencing the disruptive rather than that of prescribing the normative, as that of showing rather than saying. "Method of this work: literary montage. I have nothing to say—only to show."[16]

II

Early reviewers and critics of W. G. Sebald's books have not been slow to notice the burden of sadness carried by his form of literary attention to life. Something in human life is not going well. Disruption, distraction, threat, and anxiety—all modes of failing easily to settle in routines of given cultural life—are all but omnipresent. Anthony Lane calls attention to Sebald's focusing on the happenstantial, on whatever disrupts smoothness of emplotment, in remarking that Sebald "raised modesty to the brink of metaphysics."[17] Susan Sontag finds in Sebald "a mind in mourning"[18] somehow on behalf of us all, for experience failing to become fully and transparently meaningful. This mind expresses itself in a "laconically evoked mental distress" that embodies "a mysterious surplus of pathos" that is "never solipsistic."[19] Franz Loquai notes that Sebald's writing is marked by a sense that "the actuality of experience is apparently not to be trusted"; that is, things that actually and effectively happen or are to happen according to life plans that a traditional plot might track are continuously being disrupted by the unplanned, the surprising, and the sheerly contingent.[20]

Frank Farrell explains the existence of disruptions in part as a result of the fact that Sebald's narrator figure (a character sometimes called W. G. Sebald) is an emigrant, as are both many of the living figures whom he encounters and many of the historical figures upon whom he reflects.[21] In addition to geographic emigration, both the narrator figure and many of those whom he encounters seem to suffer from a kind of developmental or psychic emigration. Childhood, with its parental figures superintending a round of daily rituals, has somehow been left behind, and adulthood seems to offer no relations and routines of comparable stability and sureness of significance. Sebald's world, as Farrell puts it, "is unable to incarnate the present meanings of an ongoing life because of the need for a ritualized return of what can no longer come back."[22]

One might be tempted to find either the Sebald figure or the characters whose wanderings are narrated uninteresting, on the ground

that their senses of loss and their mournings are somehow patho-
logical in being determined by a failure to form stable adult attachments into which most people need not and do not fall. But exactly
how clear is it that we genuinely do better in a world dominated by
getting and spending, commodity exchange, cultural slippage, and
the fragmentation of work? Sebald's figures occupy "a world of ruins
and absences, with no features immanent to it that suggest any possibility of renewal."[23] If we reject the relevance to us of this world
and the figures within it, then we shall have somehow to sustain a
sense of the existence immanently within our world of features that
do suggest renewal, and that is not obviously so easy to do.

Mark R. McCulloh focuses similarly on Sebald's sense of outsid-
erliness in the face of cultural habits that seem to lack significance.
"What Sebald does is display openly, from the perspective of a wan-
dering outsider who happens to have certain literary leanings, the
very oddness of people, of history and its calamities, of the very pre-
dicament of being alive. Sebald's subject . . . is in the last analysis the
unsettling strangeness of the familiar."[24] In the face of this unsettling
strangeness, the best that one can do, Sebald suggests, is to bear witness to it and to the traumas that somehow lie behind it. This witness, however, includes a sense, as in Benjamin, that traumas are
intrinsic to historical life as such; no overcoming of trauma through
either political revolution or cognition is available. Sebald himself as
a critic characterized the work of the early twentieth-century German novelist Alfred Döblin as offering "an exact illustration of the
new concept of history, which is not based on the idea of progress, as
the old bourgeois concept was, but on the notion of self-perpetuating
catastrophe."[25]

Eric L. Santner describes a "'poetics of exposure' that would become
the signature style and method of Sebald's fiction."[26] Human subjects
are exposed to damage, trauma, loss, and in general to failures to
form stable and fulfilling attachments. The lives of human subjects
hence seem to have something in common with certain other "privileged materials and objects" that recur in Sebald's fiction: "dust, ash,
moth, bones, flayed skin, silk."[27] Disintegration, fragility, and decay

are substantially more prominent than integration, construction, and progress, both for human subjects and for material things.

Santner traces Sebald's poetics of exposure, sense of the fragility of human life, and feeling for the pervasiveness of trauma in history both to the conditions of subject or ego formation in general and to the specific shape of those conditions in late commodity society. He suggests that Sebald shares Benjamin's sense of our "irreducible exposure to the violence of history."[28] This exposure makes allegory (or at least the kind of deliberately overstylized, ritualized, "bald," antieschatological, unparsable allegory characteristic of the seventeenth-century German Trauerspiel as Benjamin understood it) "the symbolic mode proper to"[29] our experience, and it makes melancholy—lingering in a persistent sense of damage, trauma, and loss—the appropriate tonality for serious writing that would register the deepest tenor of human experience.

Santner argues that the continuing presence of trauma in human life in such a way that only damaged, outsiderly, less than wholehearted subjects are formed is due initially to the basis of civilization in the renunciation of parricide, as Freud described that basis in *Totemism and Taboo*. There is originally, at least for adolescent male subjects, a primordial impulse to parricide, so that they may displace the primal father in the tribe and come to enjoy a position of unrivaled possession and enjoyment of its women. At some point, however, this parricidal impulse is renounced for the sake of social peace but therein also displaced and continued in a distorted form. "The *renunciation* of the parricidal impulse (along with the fantasy of absolute jouissance entailed by the yearned-for position of the primal father) can be fully sustained only by a *compulsion to enjoy* that same impulse, though at the significant symbolic remove of ritual performance."[30] Given this renunciation and remove, male subjects come to exist in a damaged state of both permanent excitation and dissatisfaction. "The primal horde pattern [of actual slaying of the primal father] and its 'mythic violence' are in some sense both sustained and suspended *in the same stroke*"[31] with the introduction of settled civilization, superego formation and the renunciations it entails, and the law. With their lives as subjects founded on renunciations overlying excitations and unsatisfied wishes for perfect enjoyment, (male) subjects are incapable of full and stable enjoyments, and they perpetuate violence and trauma through their rivalries and competitive pursuits of objects that are in the end always in some measure unsatisfying. Open murder is renounced, but rivalry is not.

The damage continually wrought on and by (male) subjects is then exacerbated by life in modern commodity society, which displays a "paradoxical mixture of deadness and excitation, stuckness and agitation," a "nihilistic vitality," and "surplus excitation and agitation."[32] (Compare Wordsworth on the Bartholomew Fair: a "perpetual whirl of / Of trivial objects, melted and reduced / To one identity, by differences / That have no meaning, and no end"[33] and Hegel on Civil Society: "particularity . . . indulging itself in all directions as it satisfies its needs, contingent arbitrariness, and subjective caprice [so that it] destroys itself and its substantial concept in the act of enjoyment . . . infinitely agitated and continually dependent on external contingency.")[34] Nor are nonmale subjects freed from the circuits of damage that result from surplus excitation and agitation. In a world that contains circuits of damage and in which commodity production, acquisition, and exchange have displaced stable social relations and rituals, it is difficult for anyone to grow up into accomplished subjectivity bound up in stable and meaningful commitments.

It is no accident, then, that Santner wonders, against the background of this story about the development and plights of contemporary subjectivity, whether there is any room, in either the contemporary world or in Sebald's conception of it, for "a shift in subjective dispositions"[35] that might result in more meaningful life. The prospects are not on the face of it encouraging.

Sebald is utterly uninterested in what we might call the "new age" solutions to the dilemma, that is, the various therapies and techniques that proliferate throughout contemporary culture for reducing stress, enhancing well-being, and optimizing the pleasure/reality principle—in a word, for *soothing* the agitations of creaturely life. The relevant question with respect to Sebald is whether his way of constructing our historical situation leaves open the possibility of an event, a radical shift of perspective whereby something genuinely new could emerge.[36]

Santner himself offers two interrelated suggestions in response to this question. Building on work by Jonathan Lear on the possibilities of achieving a good enough psychoanalytic cure, that is, of coming to be able, as Freud is supposed to have remarked, "to work and to love," Santner proposes that it is sometimes possible "to catch a lucky break in life," that is, to become able to "appropriate the 'the possibilities for new possibilities' that are, as [Lear] puts it, 'breaking out all the time.'"[37] Building on late work by Jacques Lacan, Santner adds that the possibility of a lucky break in forming relations to other subjects may be significantly held open by the fact that women, though shaped in part by traumas attendant upon subject formation, are, in Lacan's term, "Not all," "not wholly determined by [the phallic function]."[38] As a result, there are modes of enjoyment and of investment in activity and in subject-subject relations open to women that are not so readily available to male subjects. They may have more diffuse enjoyments and investments in activity and in relationships that are not so obsessively marked by rivalry and the playing out of displaced aggression, and human subjects in general may hope that such enjoyments and investments may spread out more widely within both personal and social life.

The suggestion that the miracle of a lucky break might happen, specifically that it might happen through the agency of women in forming other modes of subject-subject relation, is by no means unimportant, and it perhaps captures well the sort of forward-looking adaptiveness in forming and maintaining relationships that figures in the personal and occupational affairs of relatively normal and happy people. When it comes to Sebald, however, this suggestion faces a number of difficulties. Though chance and coincidence abound, relatively happy, forward-looking characters capable of adaptation do not much figure in Sebald's fiction. Nor are women much present in his writings, and anything resembling a marriage plot is entirely absent. Nor does this suggestion by itself capture the work of Sebald's style and form of attention to life, which remain considerably more melancholic than celebratory of luck. Most important, this suggestion does not really address either the continuing dynamics of trauma that underlie subject formation within settled social life or the particular shape those dynamics have taken in advanced commodity society.

Santner's second suggestion builds on Terry Eagleton's reading of Benjamin, who likewise addressed the problem of "the possibility of an event." In response to the plights of subject development in contemporary life, we might, Eagleton proposes, either regress to an imaginary past, remain marooned in melancholia, or somehow, while remembering the traumatic, nonetheless "re-channel desire from both past and present to the future: to detect in the decline of the aura the form of new social and libidinal relations, realizable by revolutionary practice."[39] This suggestion, however, raises the questions of exactly how the rechanneling of desire is possible and whether Sebald's works present any plausible models for such a rechanneling. Just how and where are the forms of new social and libidinal relations to be detected? There is no hint of any turn toward revolutionary praxis in Sebald. Nor do any rechannelings of desire seem visibly present in the itineraries of Sebald's principal figures, unless, somehow, something like this, in a muted form, is accomplished within the consciousness of the narrator figure. This narrator figure manages somehow to go on with life, despite an omnipresent melancholy and consciousness of trauma, and it is possible that the possibility of going on is thereby somehow opened up to us as well. And here Santner suggests that there is in Sebald's writing "the performance of acts of witnessing" that express a "love of neighbor" that functions as "the 'miraculous' opening of a social link" first between the narrator figure and those whom he encounters and then, further, between us and like figures in our worlds.[40] This love of neighbor in the form of witness offers us "the resources for intervening in and supplementing the superego bind"[41] that haunts subject formation and that motivates the perpetuation of trauma.

The acts of witnessing Sebald carries out in and through his narrator figure are not simply a journalistic reporting of evident injury, loss, and suffering. Daily newspapers and local television news reports are already replete with such reportings, and they function within the commodity space of news reporting more to titillate, entertain, and numb their audiences than to mobilize fullness of attention. Instead, Santner argues, Sebald's attention to life takes the form of what Benjamin called "*erstarrte Unruhe*, petrified unrest."[42] Like the figure of the halted traveler in Wordsworth, or like Rilke frozen before the commanding sculpture of Apollo's torso, the narrator figure finds himself stopped and plunged into reflection and feeling. Attention is suddenly held all but obsessively by something simultaneously strange and indecipherable yet altogether ordinary.

This combination of strangeness and indecipherability with ordinariness is the signature of the uncanny (*das Unheimliche*) as Freud conceived of it. Sebald himself quotes and endorses Benjamin's remark that "histrionic or fanatical stress on the mysterious side of the mysterious takes us no further; we penetrate the mystery only to the degree that we recognize it in the everyday world."[43] Mark McCulloh observes that "it is this restoration of a sense of the uncanny (as well as of the sublime) to everyday experience that accounts for much of Sebald's appeal."[44] To see something—something strange, indecipherable, and yet strangely familiar within the ordinary—and then to dwell on this something in reflection—not to explain it, but to follow and play out the sense of strangeness, familiarity, and significance—is to reanimate one's sense of life as a human subject. It is to remind oneself, in detail, that one is capable of noticing and feeling and of sustaining attention to the strange phenomena of life in time. Such a reminder joins the narrator figure with those whom he encounters who have suffered traumas of which they are uncannily reminded and also with readers who are brought to their own sense of the presence of the traumatic and of the strangely familiar within their lives.

This form of attention to human life is a small thing. It is not an explicit praxis of economic or political-institutional life, it is neither the achievement of a happy marriage or partner-relation nor the story of one, and it is not therapy that immediately adjusts one to a workplace or to family life. But it is a small thing that might run through and renovate any of the politicoeconomic praxes, human relationships, or modes of work and family life one might take up. Without the reanimation of subject attention, there is only compulsive repetition, unthinking habit, surpluses of excitation and agitation, anomie, and dullness. With it there is a chance to lead a human life more actively, more expressively, and with more wholeheartedness of interest.

III

It is not easy to characterize stylistically, formally, technically, or linguistically the nature of the fullness of attention some writers achieve and in which we can participate by reading. Different works written in different historical circumstances and with different subject matters will have strikingly different ways formally to achieve fullness of attention. One way, however, to begin a characterization is to note the differences of fullness of literary attention from both theorizing or discursive-classificatory thinking that makes use of preexistent categories, on the one hand, and more or less instantaneous intuition or perception, on the other. This, in fact, is exactly how Benjamin, is his masterpiece essay "The Concept of Criticism in German Romanticism,"[45] both explains and extends Friedrich Schlegel's conception of the achievement of literature as an art. Schlegel, Benjamin writes, found it

> necessary . . . to seek a mediation between discursive thinking and intellectual intuition, since the one did not satisfy his imperative of intuitive comprehension, whereas the other failed to satisfy his systematic interests. He thus found himself . . . faced with the problem of combining the maximum systematic range of thought with the most extreme truncation of discursive thinking. . . . He searches for a noneidetic intuition of the system, and he finds this in language. (139–140)

The system in question here is the system of achieved freedom or of a more fully human way of life, involving full and stable care, reflection, and investment in activity. To say that intellectual intuition fails to satisfy an interest in this system is to say that such a way of life is not simply there to be grasped in either an instantaneous intellectual intuition of the whole or in a moment of blinding perception of the actual. But more temporally extended discursive-theoretic characterization of such a way of life remains, for Schlegel, abstract, or something whose availability and worth we are unable to feel directly. So one needs not a theory of freedom, the right or the good, but a more intuitive yet also temporally extended comprehension, achieved in relation to feeling, of what is possible and valuable for us.

Schlegel, then, described a certain use of language as a vehicle of attention in the successful literary work. The task of criticism is to follow and participate in the deployment of attention within the work. In so conceiving of criticism, Benjamin argues,

> Schlegel's concept of criticism achieve[d] freedom from heteronomous aesthetic doctrines, [and] it made this freedom possible in the first place by setting up for artworks a criterion other than the rule—namely, the criterion of an immanent structure specific to the work itself. He did this not with the general concepts of harmony and organization which, in the case of Herder or Moritz, were incapable of establishing a criticism of art, but with a genuine theory of art . . . as a medium of reflection and of the work as a center of reflection. (155)

There are, that is to say, no a priori knowable forms, use of which is either necessary or sufficient for success in art. Nor is there any definite content that is required. As Benjamin remarks, "the concept of measure is remote from Romanticism, which paid no heed to an a priori of content, something to be measured in art" (184). Instead, "the value of a work depends solely on whether it makes its immanent critique possible or not" (159), that is, on whether it

supports critical or readerly participation in its deployments of attention. Benjamin himself argues that this conception of the value
of a work of art remains dominant for us today, even where it is
contested by either staler classicisms, on the one hand, or by the
vulgarizations of commodity valuation and psychobiographic cults
of personality, on the other. Citing Flaubert and the Stefan George
circle, Benjamin claims that "the doctrine that art and its works are
essentially neither appearances of beauty nor manifestations of immediately inspired emotions, but media of forms, resting in themselves, has not fallen into oblivion since the Romantics, at least not
in the spirit of artistic development itself" (177), where the forms
in question are not those of classical rules or unities but forms of
fuller attention.

Form, then, does the work of reflection or of attention that blends
thought with feeling.

> Form is the objective expression of the reflection proper to
> the work, the reflection that constitutes its essence. Form is
> the possibility of reflection in the work. It grounds the work
> a priori, therefore, as a principle of existence; it is through its
> form that the work of art is a living center of reflection. In the
> medium of reflection in art, new centers of reflection are con-
> tinually forming. . . . The infinitude of art attains to reflection
> first of all only in such a center, as in a limiting value; that is,
> it attains to self-comprehension and therewith to comprehen-
> sion generally. This limit-value is the form of presentation
> [*Darstellungsweise*]⁴⁶ of the individual work. On it rests the
> possibility of a relative unity and closure of the work in the
> medium of art, [even though] the work remains burdened
> with a moment of contingency.   (156)

The relative unity and closure that Benjamin has in mind differ
from the putatively absolute closure of a demonstrative argument, on
the one hand, and the lack of closure that characterizes the merely incidental or episodic, on the other. Instead, the author's attention and

interest are excited by an initiating scene or incident. In and through the act of writing, the writer imagines what might further happen, or what thoughts and feelings are in play in relation to the initiator, as well as how, exactly, to work out in words the presentation of initiator, consequents, and attendant thoughts and feelings. A material form of presentation is here achieved in relation to the initiator, as an immanent structure rather than as form imposed from without. A center of reflection is formed in the work in relation to the initiator. The relative closure and unity of the work are achieved when attention calms itself in a feeling of completeness, signaled in a sense that "yes, it was all so." (Compare Herbert Marcuse's discussion of aesthetic unity, understood as culminating in the sense that "*Es war doch so schön*"[47]—it was all so beautiful anyway; it made sense; the work has clarified the initiating scene, even in the absence of complete system of freedom, theory of value, or demonstrated moral.)

Certain claims about the proper way of reading a literary work follow immediately from the conception of it as a material form of presentation of energies of attention, focused on an initiator and its consequents, in relation to further thoughts and feelings, in the face of the persistent onwardness of life. As Schlegel himself observed in his critique of Goethe's *Wilhelm Meister*, "it is fine and necessary to abandon oneself utterly to the impression a poetic work makes . . . and perhaps only in particular cases to confirm one's feeling through reflection and to raise it to the level of thought . . . and complete it. But it is no less necessary to be able to abstract from all that is particular, so that—hovering—one grasps the universal" (as cited in Benjamin, 153).[48] In reading, a certain abandonment to the literary text—to its energies, forms, and movements of attention—will be necessary, as one follows reflection in the process of forming itself. But it will also be necessary sometimes, intermittently, to stand back in one's own reflections, so as to balance the movement of thought one has followed against life itself, as one reflects on it, and against other courses of embodied reflection. Within these two movements of reading and with the work and its writer one can then, sometimes, for a time, come to say and feel, "yes, it was all so."

IV

In order to track and grasp more concretely this mode of conclusion and its manner of achievement through literary form, we may turn to a particular case, W. G. Sebald's long story "Paul Bereyter," the second of his four long stories published together as *The Emigrants*.[49] Like the other stories in this collection, "Paul Bereyter" focuses on its single titular character, in this case as that character is considered by a first-person narrator who had once been Paul's student in grammar school. It is a kind of muted elegy or meditation, opening with the lines: "In January 1984, the news reached me from S that on the evening of the 30th of December, a week after his seventy-fourth birthday, Paul Bereyter, who had been my teacher at primary school, had put an end to his life. A short distance from S, where the railway track curves out of a willow copse into the open fields, he had lain himself down in front of a train" (27/41).

This first sentence already embodies Sebald's striking personal style, somewhat more natural in German than in English. It begins with a prepositional phrase, the main verb is in the passive voice, two time indications delay the appearance of the noun subject "Paul Bereyter" of the main dependent clause that gives the news, and again a relative clause stands between that subject-noun phrase and its verb phrase. The second sentence continues the interrupting focus on details, as two place indications, the second in explicatory apposition to the first and offering the perceptible details of the curving track and the willow copse, precede an independent clause in the past perfect. In the German, in fact, these two sentences are one long sentence, with the dramatic "sich . . . vor den Zug legte" coming only at the very end. In addition, the clauses in German are connected by explicatory conjunctions that the English omits: "*thus* a week after his 74th birthday" ("also eine Woche nach seinem 74. Geburtstag") and "in that he had . . ." ("*indem* er sich"). The railway line leads itself out in a curve ("in einem Bogen . . . herausführt") and then attains the open field ("das offene Feld gewinnt") almost as though it, too, were a character. These two sentences are accompanied by a somewhat blurry black-and-white photograph, showing in the foreground, where it occupies about half of the picture plane at its front edge, a single rail, with to the far right edge a dark companion rail curving along with it toward the right, away from trees on the left and toward a field. It is all, already, almost unbearably evocative and melancholy. The effect of the style and the photograph is one of delay *in* details that, we may presume, have some significance in holding the narrator's attention, though this significance is not spelled out: rather, these details are to accumulate—both in the narrator's consciousness and in the consciousness of we who follow his consciousness—until they form a pattern whose significance can almost, but not quite, be explicated in a moral or secret key to the story. Instead of a moral or secret key, what the narrator gets, and what we get, is a more nearly unverbalizable sense of the pattern and of the pathos, and the beauty and fragility amid the pathos, that this life (Paul Bereyter's life) and human life (both the narrator's life and our lives) all embody.

Following this opening sentence, the narrative plays out in this style through roughly nine further scenes, as the narrator attempts to come to terms with Paul Bereyter's life, more or less as follows.

(1) The narrator notes that the obituary in the local newspaper from S fails to mention "that Paul Bereyter had died of his own free-will" (*aus freien Stücken*) (27/42) and that, besides describing his dedication to his pupils, his inventiveness as a teacher, and his love of music, it "added, with no further explanation [*In einer weiter nicht erläuterten Bemerkung*], that during the Third Reich Paul Bereyter had been prevented from practicing his chosen profession" (27/42). As a result of the manner of death and of "this curiously uncon-nected, inconsequential statement" ("Diese gänzlich unverbundene und unverbindliche Feststellung") (27/42), the narrator concerns himself more and more with Paul Bereyter ("mich . . . immer häufiger mit Paul Bereyter beschäftige"), resolving to "get beyond" his own fond memories of him in order to find out more about his secret history.

(2) The narrator returns to S, where he has been only occasion-ally since leaving school, in order to visit Paul's apartment and to

talk with the villagers. He remembers how the students, like everyone else in the village, had spoken of their teacher simply as "Paul" (28/43), and he imagines Paul lying on his balcony, skating in winter, and stretched out on the track (29/44). Or, rather, "I saw him on the airy balcony, his face vaulted over by the host of stars" ("Ich sah ihn liegen auf dem geschindelten Altan, seiner sommerlichen Schlafstatt, das Gesicht überwolbt von den Heerzügen der Gestirne") (29/44). These investigations and imaginings, however, do not bring him any closer to Paul, except in a few "emotional moments that seemed presumptuous to me" ("in gewissen Ausuferungen des Gefühls [overflowings of feelings], wie sie mir unzulässig [inadmissible, forbidden] erscheinen") (29/45). As a result, he has now written down "what I know of Paul Bereyter" ("zu deren Vermeidung ich jetzt aufgeschrieben habe, was ich von Paul Bereyter weiß und im Verlauf meiner Erkundigen über ihn in Erfahrung bringen konnte") (29/45).

(3) The narrator describes his family's move from W to S, "19 kilometers away" (32/45), and his joining Paul Bereyter's third class. He recalls his friendship with Fritz Binswanger, a slow boy who exactly shared the narrator's "incorrigibly sloppy handwriting" ("unverbesserlich schweinisch Handschrift") (31/47). They study cockchafer beetles together and share lunches. Once they each receive a present of "a white butterpear" (32/49). Fritz later became a chef of "international renown" (32/49). The narrator and Fritz later meet in London, in 1984, "in the reading room of the British Museum, where I was researching the history of Bering's Alaska expedition and Fritz was studying eighteenth-century French cookbooks" (32/49).

(4) The narrator describes the layout of the classroom in S, with "twenty-six desks screwed fast to the oiled floorboards" (33/50–51). A sketch accompanies this description. Paul's bearing and teaching style are described. He often stood not at the front but "in one of the window bays towards the head of the room half facing the class and half turned to look out, his face at a slightly upturned angle with the sunlight glinting on his glasses; and from that position he would talk across to us" (34/52). He spoke "in well-structured sentences"

"without any touch of dialect but with a slight impediment of speech or timbre, as if the sound were coming not from the larynx but from somewhere near the heart" (34–35/52). Paul's freethinking in religion and his "aversion to hypocrisy of any description" ("die Abneigung Pauls gegen alles Scheinheilige") are described (36/55). He did not attend church. Instead of using the prescribed text, he taught from a collection of stories, "the *Rheinische Hausfreund*" (37/56) that he "had procured, I suspect at his own expense" (37/56–57). He spoke fluent French. He emphasized natural history, and he often took the class on visits to interesting sites: a brewery, a gunsmith's, a castle, and an abandoned coal mine. He played the clarinet and was strikingly good at whistling, favoring melodies that the narrator only later recognized as by Brahms and Bellini (41/61). He once brought to the class a young conservatory violinist, and Paul was "far from being able to hide the emotion that [the] playing produced in him [and] had to remove his glasses because his eyes had filled with tears" (41/62). Often "he might stop or sit down somewhere, alone and apart from us all, as if he, who was always in good spirits and seemed so cheerful, was in fact desolation itself" ("die Untröstlichkeit selber") (42/62). This teaching style, and these and other incidents, are strikingly close to what we know of Wittgenstein's career as a rural schoolteacher, and Wittgenstein is mentioned later in the text.

(5) The narrator describes what he has learned about Paul from Lucy Landau, who now lives in the Villa Bonlieu in Yverdon, Switzerland, and who had arranged Paul's burial in S. Since his retirement from teaching in 1971, Paul had mostly lived in Yverdon. He and Lucy had met each other at Salin-les-Bains in the French Jura, where she had been reading Nabokov's autobiography on a park bench (43/65). Some of Lucy's own childhood in Switzerland is recounted. Paul had explained to her in Salin-les-Bains that his "condition" and his "claustrophobia" had now made him unable to teach (43/65). His condition included now seeing "his pupils, although he had always felt affection for them (he stressed this), as contemptible and repulsive creatures [*verächtliche und hassenswerte Kreaturen*], the very sight of whom had prompted an utterly groundless violence

in him on more than one occasion" that he had felt break out in him (43–44/65–66). Paul, we are told Lucy said, "was almost consumed by the loneliness within him [*von seiner inneren Einsamkeit nahezu aufgefressenen*]," though he was "the most considerate and entertaining companion one could wish for" (44/66–67). In conversation, Paul "had linked the bourgeois concept of Utopia and order . . . with the progressive destruction of natural life" (45/67). She herself, when gazing with Paul at Lake Geneva from the top of Montrond, "had for the first time in her life . . . a sense of the contrarieties that are in our longings" ("die widersprüchlichen Dimensionen unserer Sehnsucht") (45/68). Lucy explains to the narrator that Paul had earlier lived in France, from 1935 to 1939, and she gives the narrator an album of photographs and notes, kept by Paul, that covers "almost the whole of [his] life" (45/68).

(6) The narrator reports that "since then I have returned to [the album] time and time again, because, looking at the pictures in it, it truly seemed to me, and still does, as if the dead were coming back, or as if we were on the point of joining them" (46/68–69). Various photographs from the album are reproduced in the narrator's story we are reading. The album and the photos tell of "a happy childhood" (46/69) and years "in a country boarding school" (46/69). Paul had submitted to the narrow-minded and morbidly Catholic demands of a teacher training school solely in order to be able to teach children (46–47/69). In the summer following a year of probationary teaching in S in 1934–1935, Paul spent a good deal of time with Helen Hollaender from Vienna, "an independent-spirited, clever woman" whose "waters ran deep" and in which "Paul liked to see his own reflection" (48/72), at least as Mme. Landau interprets the photographs to the narrator. In autumn 1935, Paul took up a teaching post "in the remote village of W" but was almost immediately dismissed "because of the new laws" (48/72). Meanwhile, Helen had returned with her mother to Vienna, from where "there could be little doubt that Helen and her mother had been deported, in one of those special trains that left Vienna at dawn, probably to Theresienstadt in the first instance" (40–50/73).

(7) Paul too, Mme. Landau reports to the narrator, is one-quarter Jewish, the grandson of the Jewish merchant Amschel Bereyter from Gunzenhausen in Franconia, and the son of Theodor, who had trained in a department store in Nuremberg before opening his own shop in S (50–51/75). "In his childhood," Mme. Landau reports Paul to have said,

> everything in the emporium seemed far too high up for him, doubtless because he himself was small, but also because the shelves reached all the four metres up to the ceiling. The light in the emporium, coming through the small transom windows let into the tops of the display window backboards, was dim even on the brightest of days, and it must have seemed all the murkier to him as a child, Paul had said, as he moved on his tricycle, mostly on the lowest level, through the ravines between tables, boxes and counters, amidst a variety of smells—mothballs and lily-of-the-valley soap were always the most pungent, while felted wool and loden cloth assailed the nose only in wet weather, herrings and linseed oil in hot. (51/76)

Paul's father Theo died of a heart attack on Palm Sunday, 1936, but perhaps also from "the fury and fear that had been consuming him, ever since, precisely two years before his death, the Jewish families, resident in his home town of Gunzenhausen for generations, had been the target of violent attacks" (53/79). Even though it "could not be 'Aryanized'" officially, the shop had nevertheless to be sold for "next to nothing," and Paul's mother Thela "died within a few weeks" (53–54/79–80).

(8) After it became "no longer tenable" (55/81) for him as a German to serve as a tutor in France, Paul returned to Berlin in 1939 to work at an office job in a garage. A few months later he was called up, and he spent six years in the motorized artillery, serving on all three fronts. Under one photograph of himself from this period, Paul wrote that "day by day, hour by hour, with every beat of the pulse, one

lost more and more of one's qualities, became less comprehensible to oneself, increasingly abstract" (56/83). In 1945, "a German to the marrow" ("von Grund auf") (57/84), Paul returned to S, "which in fact he loathed . . . said Mme. Landau" (57/84), again to teach. He "spent a lot of time gardening" (57/85). During this time, he read "Altenberg, Trakl, Wittgenstein, Friedell, Hasenclever, Toller, Tucholsky, Klaus Mann, Ossietzky, Benjamin, Koestler, and Zweig: almost all of them writers who had taken their own lives or been close to doing so" (58/86). He "copied out hundreds of pages" into his notebooks, "time and again . . . stories of suicides" (58/86), as though to convince himself "that he belonged to the exiles and not to the people of S" (59/87–88). He retired in 1971 and thereafter lived principally in Yverdon, near Mme. Landau, where he devoted himself to his gardening and reading.

(9) In 1982, Paul's vision once again began to deteriorate. In autumn 1983, he informed Lucy that he wished to give up his flat in S. "Not long after Christmas" (60/89), they traveled to S together to settle affairs. "No snow had fallen, there was no sign anywhere of any winter tourism. . . . On the third day a spell of mild *föhn* weather set in, quite unusual for the time of year. The pine forests were black on the mountainsides, the windows gleamed like lead, and the sky was so low and dark one expected ink to run out of it any moment" (60–61/89–90). While Mme. Landau was sleeping in the afternoon from a headache, Paul went out. Upon being informed of his death, she thought of the railway timetables and directories he had collected and of "the Märklin model railway he had laid" (61/91) out in his rooms. Hearing this, the narrator thinks of "the stations, tracks, goods depots and signal boxes" that he had as a child to copy from the blackboard in Paul's classroom (61/91). Paul had told Mme. Landau of a summer holiday in his own childhood that he had spent watching trains pass "from the mainland to the island and from the island to the mainland" (62/92). At that time, Paul's uncle had said he would "end up on the railways" ("bei der Eisenbahn enden") (63/92). Though this struck her as "darkly foreboding" ("er hatte auf mich die dunkle Wirkung eines Orakelspruchs") (63/93), Mme. Landau reported that "the disquiet I

experienced lasted only a very short time, and passed over me like the shadow of a bird in flight" ("ging über mich hinweg wie der Schatten eines Vogels im Flug") (63/93).

V

The action of this story, like the action of lyric, takes place entirely in memory, within the consciousness of the narrator and in the past tense. Also like lyric, the overall structural pattern of the story is out-in-out. That is, an initiating scene or incident in the world (here the news of Paul Bereyter's suicide and the subsequent newspaper account of it) prompts a course of memory, reflection, and further action, all of which are then recollected in the past tense of the narrative itself. The narrative then ends with a turn again out toward the world—the image of Mme. Landau reporting the passing over her of her disquiet—so as to let the world go its own way.

The recollective actions and attentions of the narrator model for us our attentions to details of our own lives, as we too seem sometimes to haunt the world, from within our reserves of loneliness, yet also seem sometimes to be bound up in things, without any clear sense of the forces or logic of loneliness and activity. As in lyric, we participate in the narrator's own recollections and attentions. In the case of the sixteen photographs and diagrams that appear within the story, we literally see what the narrator sees. The photographs and diagrams are chosen and placed by the author (who may or may not be the narrator), and it is not clear that they are in each case documentary in relation to the incidents of the story. Sometimes they seem documentary; sometimes they seem more general than that, to be deposited more for the sake of a mood or tonality that they evoke in relation to incidents than out of a documentary intention. This ambiguity heightens the sense of the uncanny and of "unseen affinities" between narrated events and some felt but scarcely verbalizable significances.

Similarly, the narrator himself, and we through the narrator, sometimes seem to see and feel what Paul or Lucy see and feel, especially, for example, in the long description of the details of Theo

Bereyter's emporium, with its high windows, dim light, and pungent smells. It is easy for us here to recall the fuguelike actions of play (riding a tricycle down the aisles) and seemingly giant scale of objects of our own childhoods. And yet, stopped by the photographs, we seem sometimes to be thrown back on ourselves, seem to see only their mysteriously evocative black on white, detached from any narrative arc. With the narrator, and perhaps with anyone who reflects, we find ourselves left outside the plot, if there is a plot at all.

A philosophical or theological theory might hope to describe the essence of the situation that we share, to some extent, with Paul, Lucy, and the narrator. A political or sexual history might hope to sort out and explain the relative influences on Paul, and on us, of Jewishness (or another religion) or of sexual longing of one or another shape, subsuming Paul and us under its generalizations. Such descriptions and generalizations might be apt. But something nonetheless would be missed in them: the intimate detail and density of consciousness and its movements in perception, as it finds itself now in this situation, now in that, struck by surprises and intensities that seem to resist full capture by either essential descriptions or subsumptive generalizations. A task of literature—or at least of this kind of intensely lyrical and elegiac literature—is to render some of these movements for our identification, thus enabling us, along with their narrators (and writers) to work them through, so as to be all at once ourselves, in our particular personalities, lonelinesses, and intensities of perception and recollection, and also in the world, able, in the end, to let it go its own way, with an appropriate sense of mystery and wonder at it, and at how one has been in it, but not, quite, ever altogether of it. The movement of working through is as important or more important than the events that are narrated. Sebald's literary technique heightens our awareness of this through his continual use of devices of interruption: narratively through shifts from the narrator's own investigations, to what Mme. Landau said, to what is actually in Paul's album; syntactically through the interjection of prepositional and appositional phrases, piling up details for perception, in between noun phrase subjects and verbs. These details invite reflections, both historical and philosophical; were there no such invitations, we would encounter only the incidental or episodic. But reflection is not allowed to settle into any definite metaphysical, sociohistorical, or psychoanalytic systems for interpretation. (One must, as Schlegel remarked, both abandon oneself to the poetry of the text and hover above it, seeking the universal. New centers of reflection are continually forming.) This kind of literature presents for our working through what this story has itself called "a sense of the contrarieties that are in our longings" ("die widersprüchlichen Dimensionen unserer Sehnsucht") (45/68), as we ourselves move through its details and in doing so reflect on them.

The story "Paul Bereyter" is headed by a motto, "Manche Nebelflecken löset kein Auge auf," well enough translated as "There is mist that no eye can dispel" (25/39). In fact, however, this motto is a quotation from a quite special context: Jean Paul's *Vorschule der Ästhetik*, part 1, section 3, paragraph 14, entitled "Instinct of Genius or the Matter of Genius" ("Instinkt des Genies oder genialer Stoff"). The full passage runs as follows:

> Many godlike spirits have been impressed by destiny with a grotesque [*unförmliche*] form, as Socrates had the body of a satyr; for time governs the form, but not the inner matter. Thus the poetic mirror with which Jakob Böhme rendered heaven and earth hung in a dark place; also in some places the glass lacks the foil. In this way the great Hamann is a deep heaven full of telescopic stars, and some nebula spots [*Nebelflecken*] no eye can penetrate.[50]

The immediate sense here is that Hamann's deep writings, writings that capture as it were the whole world and Hamann the man himself, have features that no one can understand. Discursive thought, seeking essential descriptions and subsumptive generalizations, will miss at least something of what they contain and present. These somethings can at best be looked on from a certain distance and with a certain awareness of one's own incomprehension. In the phrase "in a dark place" ("in einem dunklen Orte"), there is a further distant echo of Dante's "in a dark wood" in the opening lines of the *Inferno*:

> Midway through this way of life we're bound upon,
> I woke to find myself in a dark wood,
> Where the right road was wholly lost and gone.[51]

We lead our lives in time and as finite subjects, where the relations between the form (the social shape) of a life and the internal matter (one's particular personality, feeling, and longing) remain always, to some extent, other than transparent. This lack of transparency shows itself especially in certain perplexing, initiating scenes and incidents and then in the emotionally modulating reflections that follow them, as one seeks in reflection more transparency, a better fit, or fuller attention—until in the end life is allowed to go on, on its own. Literature—some literature, this lyric literature of Sebald's—knows this and makes it manifest for us. To see and feel this, and to see and feel it in detail, through perception and accompanying reflection, is to be, in a certain way, more fully seduced to life.

Appendix

Lines Composed a Few Miles Above Tintern Abbey, on Revisiting the Banks of the Wye During a Tour, July 13, 1798

William Wordsworth

Five years have passed; five summers, with the length
Of five long winters! and again I hear
These waters, rolling from their mountain-springs
With a soft inland murmur.—Once again
Do I behold these steep and lofty cliffs,   5
That on a wild secluded scene impress
Thoughts of more deep seclusion; and connect
The landscape with the quiet of the sky.
The day is come when I again repose
Here, under this dark sycamore, and view   10
These plots of cottage ground, these orchard tufts,
Which at this season, with their unripe fruits,
Are clad in one green hue, and lose themselves
'Mid groves and copses. Once again I see
These hedgerows, hardly hedgerows, little lines   15
Of sportive wood run wild; these pastoral farms,
Green to the very door; and wreaths of smoke

Sent up, in silence, from among the trees!
With some uncertain notice, as might seem
Of vagrant dwellers in the houseless woods,   20
Or of some Hermit's cave, where by his fire
The Hermit sits alone.
                      These beauteous forms,
Through a long absence, have not been to me
As is a landscape to a blind man's eye;
But oft, in lonely rooms, and 'mid the din   25
Of towns and cities, I have owed to them,
In hours of weariness, sensations sweet,
Felt in the blood, and felt along the heart;
And passing even into my purer mind,
With tranquil restoration—feelings too   30
Of unremembered pleasure; such, perhaps,
As have no slight or trivial influence
On that best portion of a good man's life,
His little, nameless, unremembered, acts
Of kindness and of love. Nor less, I trust,   35
To them I may have owed another gift,
Of aspect more sublime; that blessed mood,
In which the burthen of the mystery,
In which the heavy and the weary weight
Of all this unintelligible world,   40
Is lightened:—that serene and blessed mood,
In which the affections gently lead us on,—
Until, the breath of this corporeal frame
And even the motion of our human blood
Almost suspended, we are laid asleep   45
In body, and become a living soul;
While with an eye made quiet by the power
Of harmony, and the deep power of joy,
We see into the life of things.
                                 If this
Be but a vain belief, yet, oh! how oft—   50

In darkness and amid the many shapes
Of joyless daylight; when the fretful stir
Unprofitable, and the fever of the world,
Have hung upon the beatings of my heart—
How oft, in spirit, have I turned to thee,   55
O sylvan Wye! thou wanderer through the woods,
How often has my spirit turned to thee!
And now, with gleams of half-extinguished thought,
With many recognitions dim and faint,
And somewhat of a sad perplexity,   60
The picture of the mind revives again;
While here I stand, not only with the sense
Of present pleasure, but with pleasing thoughts
That in this moment there is life and food
For future years. And so I dare to hope,   65
Though changed, no doubt, from what I was when first
I came among these hills; when like a roe
I bounded o'er the mountains, by the sides
Of the deep rivers, and the lonely streams,
Wherever nature led: more like a man   70
Flying from something that he dreads than one
Who sought the thing he loved. For nature then
(The coarser pleasures of my boyish days,
And their glad animal movements all gone by)
To me was all in all.—I cannot paint   75
What then I was. The sounding cataract
Haunted me like a passion; the tall rock,
The mountain, and the deep and gloomy wood,
Their colours and their forms, were then to me
An appetite; a feeling and a love,   80
That had no need of a remoter charm,
By thought supplied, nor any interest
Unborrowed from the eye.—That time is past,
And all its aching joys are now no more,
And all its dizzy raptures. Not for this   85

Faint I, nor mourn nor murmur; other gifts
Have followed; for such loss, I would believe,
Abundant recompense. For I have learned
To look on nature, not as in the hour
Of thoughtless youth; but hearing oftentimes   90
The still, sad music of humanity,
Nor harsh nor grating, though of ample power
To chasten and subdue. And I have felt
A presence that disturbs me with the joy
Of elevated thoughts; a sense sublime   95
Of something far more deeply interfused,
Whose dwelling is the light of setting suns,
And the round ocean and the living air,
And the blue sky, and in the mind of man:
A motion and a spirit, that impels   100
All thinking things, all objects of all thought,
And rolls through all things. Therefore am I still
A lover of the meadows and the woods,
And mountains; and of all that we behold
From this green earth; of all the mighty world   105
Of eye, and ear—both what they half create,
And what perceive; well pleased to recognize
In nature and the language of the sense
The anchor of my purest thoughts, the nurse,
The guide, the guardian of my heart, and soul   110
Of all my moral being.
                                        Nor perchance,
If I were not thus taught, should I the more
Suffer my genial spirits to decay:
For thou art with me here upon the banks
Of this fair river; thou my dearest Friend,   115
My dear, dear Friend; and in thy voice I catch
The language of my former heart, and read
My former pleasures in the shooting lights
Of thy wild eyes. Oh! yet a little while

May I behold in thee what I was once,   120
My dear, dear Sister! and this prayer I make,
Knowing that Nature never did betray
The heart that loved her; 'tis her privilege,
Through all the years of this our life, to lead
From joy to joy: for she can so inform   125
The mind that is within us, so impress
With quietness and beauty, and so feed
With lofty thoughts, that neither evil tongues,
Rash judgments, nor the sneers of selfish men,
Nor greetings where no kindness is, nor all   130
The dreary intercourse of daily life,
Shall e'er prevail against us, or disturb
Our cheerful faith, that all which we behold
Is full of blessings. Therefore let the moon
Shine on thee in thy solitary walk;   135
And let the misty mountain winds be free
To blow against thee: and, in after years,
When these wild ecstasies shall be matured
Into a sober pleasure; when thy mind
Shall be a mansion for all lovely forms,   140
Thy memory be as a dwelling-place
For all sweet sounds and harmonies; oh! then,
If solitude, or fear, or pain, or grief
Should be thy portion, with what healing thoughts
Of tender joy wilt thou remember me,   145
And these my exhortations! Nor, perchance—
If I should be where I no more can hear
Thy voice, nor catch from thy wild eyes these gleams
Of past existence—wilt thou then forget
That on the banks of this delightful stream   150
We stood together; and that I, so long
A worshipper of Nature, hither came
Unwearied in that service; rather say
With warmer love—oh! with far deeper zeal

Of holier love. Nor wilt thou then forget, 155
That after many wanderings, many years
Of absence, these steep woods and lofty cliffs,
And this green pastoral landscape, were to me
More dear, both for themselves and for thy sake!

Notes

1. Introduction: Subjectivity, Modernity, and the Uses of Literature

1. If one is interested in fixing the extension of "literature" in such a way that all plausible cases are covered, one will end up with something like the radically disjunctive definition offered by Robert Stecker: "A work w is a work of literature if and only if w is produced in a linguistic medium, and, (1) w is a novel, short story, tale, drama, or poem, and the writer of w intended that it possess aesthetic, cognitive or interpretation-centered value, and the work is written with sufficient technical skill for it to be possible to take that intention seriously, or (2) w possesses aesthetic, cognitive, or interpretation-centered value to a significant degree, or (3) w falls under a predecessor concept to our concept of literature and was written while the predecessor concept held sway, or (4) w belongs to the work of a great writer" ("What is Literature?" *Revue Internationale de Philosophie* 50 [1996]: 694). This may be correct enough, but it offers little illumination about how literature achieves aesthetic, cognitive, or interpretation-centered value or about how the achievement of such values matters for human life.

2. This is roughly the view of Wayne Booth in *The Company We Keep: An Ethics of Fiction* (Berkeley: University of California Press, 1988). Books are like friends who help us to widen the range of points of view we can occupy. While this suggestion has some truth to it, it underrates the formal, cognitive, and affective intensities of literary structure and distinctively literary craft.

3. Bill Readings usefully surveys the rise and decline of the humanities within the modern university from Humboldt to the present as central disciplines devoted to teaching national literatures in *The University in Ruins* (Cambridge, Mass.: Harvard University Press, 1997).

4. Frank Ferrell, *Why Does Literature Matter?* (Ithaca, N.Y.: Cornell University Press, 2004). See 213 ff. for a summary of the "modern" developments listed in the remainder of this paragraph.

5. Ibid., 201.

6. Farrell summarizes the registers of recovery that literary works offer us on ibid., 9–19.

7. Ibid., 187.

8. Ibid., 72.

9. David E. Wellbery, *The Specular Moment: Goethe's Lyric and Early Romanticism* (Stanford, Calif.: Stanford University Press, 1996), 48.

10. The complete text of "Wilkommen und Abschied" in German and in English translation appears on 28–29 of ibid.

11. Ibid., 49.

12. Ibid.

13. Ibid., 3.

14. Eric L. Santner, *On Creaturely Life* (Chicago: University of Chicago Press, 2006), 33.

15. J. M. Bernstein, *Against Voluptuous Bodies: Late Modernism and the Meaning of Painting* (Stanford, Calif.: Stanford University Press, 2006), 45.

16. Ralph Waldo Emerson, "Circles," in *Emerson: Essays and Lectures* (New York: Viking Press, 1983), 406.

17. Jürgen Habermas, *The Philosophical Discourse of Modernity*, trans. Frederick G. Lawrence (Cambridge, Mass.: The MIT Press, 1987), 8.

18. Ibid., 9.

19. Charles Baudelaire, "The Painter of Modern Life," in Baudelaire, *Selected Writings on Art and Artists*, trans. P. E. Charvet (Harmondsworth: Penguin, 1972), 392, cited in Habermas, *The Philosophical Discourse of Modernity*, 9.

20. Bernstein, *Against Voluptuous Bodies*, 11.

21. Philip Weinstein powerfully and usefully surveys the registering of trauma and resistance to overly stable Bildungsroman plots on the parts of Kafka, Proust, and Faulkner in his *Unknowing: The Work of Modernist Fiction* (Ithaca, N.Y.: Cornell University Press, 2005).

22. Tzachi Zamir powerfully traces various forms of this slippage as they are expressed in the careers of the protagonists of the major Shakespearean tragedies in his *Double Vision: Moral Philosophy and Shakespearean Drama* (Princeton, N.J.: Princeton University Press, 2007).

23. See Michael Tomasello, *The Cultural Origins of Human Cognition* (Cambridge, Mass.: Harvard University Press, 2001), and *Constructing a Language: A Usage-Based Theory of Language Acquisition* (Cambridge, Mass.: Harvard University Press, 2005). For a summary of this work that brings it into connection with Wittgenstein's *Philosophical Investigations*, see Richard Eldridge, "Wittgenstein on Aspect-Seeing, the Nature of Discursive Consciousness, and the Experience of Agency," in *Seeing Wittgenstein Anew: New Essays on Aspect-Seeing*, ed. William Day and Victor Krebs (Cambridge: Cambridge University Press), forthcoming.

24. This is the main argument, as I read it, of Wittgenstein's *Philosophical Investigations*. See Eldridge, *Leading a Human Life: Wittgenstein, Intentionality, and Romanticism* (Chicago: University of Chicago Press, 1997).

25. J. L. Austin, "Truth," in Austin, *Philosophical Papers*, 2nd ed. (Oxford: Oxford University Press, 1970), 126 n. 1.

26. René Descartes, *The Search After Truth by the Light of Nature*, trans. E. S. Haldane and G. R. T. Ross, in *The Philosophical Works of Descartes*, ed. E. S. Haldane and G. R. T. Ross (Cambridge: Cambridge University Press, 1911), 1:305.

27. Kant, "What Is Enlightenment?" trans. Lewis White Beck, in Kant, *On History*, ed. Lewis White Beck (Indianapolis, Ind.: Bobbs-Merrill, 1963), 3 n. 1.

28. Here I follow Stanley Cavell's reading, itself developed in response to Emerson's readings of Descartes and Kant, of Descartes' account in the *Meditations* of his knowledge of his own existence. See Cavell, "Being Odd, Getting Even (Descartes, Emerson, Poe)" in Cavell, *In Quest of the Ordinary: Lines of Skepticism and Romanticism* (Chicago: University of Chicago Press, 1988), 105–130.

29. Descartes, *Meditations on First Philosophy*, in *The Philosophical Works of Descartes*, 1:150.

30. Ibid., 1:151–152.

31. Cavell, *The Senses of Walden: An Expanded Edition* (San Francisco: North Point Press, 1981), 107.

32. Henry David Thoreau, *Walden*, ed. J. Lyndon Shanley (Princeton, N.J.: Princeton University Press, 2004), 159.

33. Cavell, *The Senses of Walden*, 107–108.

34. Kant, "Idea for a Universal History from a Cosmopolitan Point of View," in Kant, *On History*, 22.

35. Kant, *Lectures on Ethics*, trans. Louis Infield (Gloucester: Peter Smith, 1978), 140.

36. Kant, "What Is Enlightenment?" 3.

37. Thomas Pfau, "The Voice of Critique: Aesthetic Cognition After Kant," part 1, in *Romantic Circles Praxis Series*, available online at http://www.rc.umd/edu/praxis/philosophy/pfau1/tp1.html.

38. Aristotle, *Poetics*, trans. Stephen Halliwell (London: Gerald Duckworth, 1987), excerpted in *The Philosophy of Art: Readings Ancient and Modern*, ed. Alex Neill and Aaron Ridly (New York: McGraw-Hill, 1995), 490. A slightly different wording appears in Aristotle, *Poetics*, trans. Stephen Halliwell, in Aristotle, *Poetics*, together with Longinus, *On the Sublime*, and Demetrius, *On Style* (Cambridge, Mass.: Harvard University Press, 1995), 37.

39. Adorno, *Negative Dialectics*, trans. E. B. Ashton (New York: Continuum, 1973), 12; emphasis and interjection added.

40. Ibid., 13.

41. Adorno, *Aesthetic Theory*, trans. Robert Hullot-Kentor (Minneapolis: University of Minnesota Press, 1997), 131.

42. Catherine Wilson, "Literature and Knowledge," *Philosophy* 58 (1983). Reprinted in *Philosophy of Literature*, ed. Eileen John and Dominic McIver Lopes (Oxford: Blackwell, 2004), 327.

43. Charles Altieri, *The Particulars of Rapture* (Ithaca, N.Y.: Cornell University Press, 2003).

44. Ludwig Wittgenstein, *Philosophical Investigations*, 2nd. ed., trans. G. E. M. Anscombe (New York: The Macmillan Company [1953], 1958), §122, 49e. See also Richard Eldridge, "Hypotheses, Criterial Claims, and Perspicuous Representations: Wittgenstein's 'Remarks on Frazer's *The Golden Bough*,'" in Eldridge, *The Persistence of Romanticism* (Cambridge: Cambridge University Press, 2001), 127–144.

45. See chapter 5, note 9.

46. Richard Eldridge, *An Introduction to the Philosophy of Art* (Cambridge: Cambridge University Press, 2003), 259 and passim.

47. Ibid., 260.

48. Wolfgang Huemer, "Introduction: Wittgenstein, Language, Philosophy of Literature," in *The Literary Wittgenstein*, ed. John Gibson and Wolfgang Huemer (London: Routledge, 2004), 5.

49. Ibid., 6–7.

50. See Spinoza, *Ethics*, in Spinoza, *Selections*, ed. John Wild (New

York: Charles Scribner's Sons, 1930), part 5, propositions 3–10, pp. 369–377. Compare also both R. G. Collingwood on artistic expression, *The Principles of Art* (Oxford: Oxford University Press, 1938), 282–283; and William Wordsworth, "Preface to Preface to *Lyrical Ballads*," in *Selected Poems and Prefaces*, ed. Jack Stillinger (Boston: Houghton Mifflin Company, 1965), 448, on how a poet may uncover "what is really important to men" through thinking "long and deeply" in relation to our feelings.

51. William Rothman and Marian Keane, *Reading Cavell's* The World Viewed (Detroit, Mich.: Wayne State University Press, 2000), 19.

52. A wonderful essay on these parallel identifications is Ted Cohen's "Identifying with Metaphor: Metaphors of Personal Identification," *The Journal of Aesthetics and Art Criticism* 57, no. 4 (1999): 399–409, on identifying with Lily Bart, Jake Gittis, and Marlowe, as well as Shakespeare, Mozart, and Conrad.

53. Plato, *Republic*, trans. G. M. A. Grube, revised C. D. C. Reeve (Indianapolis, Ind.: Hackett Publishing Company, 1992), 348b, p. 24.

2. Romanticism, Cartesianism, Humeanism, Byronism: *Stoppard's* Arcadia

1. John Dewey, *Art as Experience* (New York: Perigee, 1980 [1934]), 337–338.

2. G. W. F. Hegel, *Philosophy of Right*, trans. T. M. Knox (Oxford: Oxford University Press, 1967), §185, p. 123.

3. See Plato, *Republic*, trans. G. M. A. Grube (Indianapolis, Ind.: Hackett Publishing Company, 1992), book 7, 557a–563e, pp. 227–234.

4. Northrop Frye, *The Great Code: The Bible and Literature* (New York: Harcourt Brace Jovanovich, 1983), 5–14.

5. Rene Descartes, preface to *The Search After Truth by the Light of Nature*, in *The Philosophical Works of Descartes*, trans. Elizabeth S. Haldane and G. R. T. Ross (Cambridge: Cambridge University Press, 1931), 1:305.

6. Frye, *The Great Code*, 52.

7. Donald G. Marshall, "Foreword: Wordsworth and Post-Enlightenment Culture," in Geoffrey H. Hartman, *The Unremarkable Wordsworth* (Minneapolis: University of Minnesota Press, 1987), vii.

8. Charles Larmore, *The Romantic Legacy* (New York: Columbia University Press, 1996).

9. See, for example, G.W.F. Hegel, *Hegel's Introduction to Aesthetics*, trans. T.M. Knox (Oxford: Oxford University Press, 1979), 81.

10. See Jerome J. McGann, *The Romantic Ideology* (Chicago: University of Chicago Press, 1983).

11. David Hume, *An Enquiry Concerning Human Understanding*, ed. Eric Steinberg (Indianapolis, Ind.: Hackett Publishing Company, 1977), section 12, p. 111.

12. W.V.O. Quine, "On the Nature of Moral Values," in Quine, *Theories and Things* (Cambridge, Mass.: Harvard University Press, 1981), 61.

13. Charles Taylor, *The Sources of the Self* (Cambridge, Mass.: Harvard University Press, 1989), 151, 154.

14. Descartes, *Discourse on Method*, in *Discourse on Method and Meditations*, trans. Donald A. Cress (Indianapolis, Ind.: Hackett Publishing Company, 1980), 14.

15. Ibid., 14, 15.

16. Ibid., 13.

17. Bertrand Russell, *A History of Western Philosophy* (New York: Simon and Schuster, 1945), 747.

18. Byron, George Gordon, Baron, "Childe Harold's Pilgrimage" in *Byron's Poetry*, ed. Frank D. McConnell (New York: W.W. Norton, 1978), Canto the First, II, p. 26.

19. Ibid., Canto the First, V, p. 26.

20. *Tom Stoppard's Arcadia: A Study Guide from Gale's Drama for Students*, vol. 5, chap. 2, e-text PDF document (Farmington Hills, Mich.: The Gale Group, 2002), DOI 10.1223/GALFSDSF0000074, p. 48.

21. See Gary Gutting, *Pragmatic Liberalism and the Critique of Modernity* (Cambridge: Cambridge University Press, 1999).

22. William Wordsworth, *The Prelude* [1850], in Wordsworth, *Selected Poems and Prefaces*, ed. Jack Stillinger (Boston: Houghton Mifflin Company, 1965), XIV, 446–447, p. 366.

23. Ibid., I, 302, p. 199.

24. Ibid., II, 233–234, p. 212.

25. Wordsworth, "The Sublime and the Beautiful," in *The Prose Works of William Wordsworth*, ed. W.J.B. Owen and J.W. Smyser (Oxford: Clarendon, 1974), 2:349–360, at 2:357.

26. Wordsworth, "Essay, Supplementary to The Preface" [1815], in Wordsworth, *Selected Poems and Prefaces*, 471–481, at 477.

27. Wordsworth, *The Prelude*, IX, 8, p. 304.

28. Harold Bloom, "The Internalization of Quest Romance," in *Romanticism and Consciousness*, ed. H. Bloom (New York: W.W. Norton, 1970), 3–24.

29. Tom Stoppard, in Mel Gussow, *Conversations with Tom Stoppard* (New York: Grove Press, 1995), 91.

30. Stoppard, cited in *Tom Stoppard's Arcadia: A Study Guide from Gale's Drama for Students*, 56.

31. Stoppard, *Conversations with Tom Stoppard*, 3.

32. Ibid., 14.

33. Ibid., 74.

34. J. L. Austin, *Sense and Sensibilia* (Oxford: Oxford University Press, 1962), 2.

35. See the unfavorable review by John Simon, cited in *Tom Stoppard's Arcadia: A Study Guide from Gale's Drama for Students*, 54.

36. See the reviews cited in *Tom Stoppard's Arcadia: A Study Guide from Gale's Drama for Students*, 34, 54–55, 56, 59.

37. Tim Appelo, "Review of *Arcadia*," *The Nation*, Jan. 5, 1995, reprinted in Tom *Stoppard's Arcadia: A Study Guide from Gale's Drama for Students*, 54A.

38. Stoppard, *Arcadia* (London: Faber and Faber, 1993), II, 5, p. 62.

39. Ibid., II, 7, p. 76.

40. Ibid., II, 7, p. 84.

41. Ibid., I, 2, p. 33.

42. Ibid., II, 7, pp. 75, 76.

43. Herbert Marcuse, *The Aesthetic Dimension* (Boston: Beacon Press, 1978), 60.

44. Theodor W. Adorno, "On Lyric Poetry and Society," in Adorno, *Notes to Literature*, trans. S. W. Nicholsen (New York: Columbia University Press, 1991), 1:41.

45. Samuel Beckett, *The Unnamable*, in Beckett, *Three Novels: Molloy, Malone Dies, The Unnamable* (New York: Grove Press, 1995), 414.

3. Romantic Subjectivity in Goethe and Wittgenstein

1. See M.W. Rowe, "Goethe and Wittgenstein," *Philosophy* 66 (1991); Joachim Schulte, "Chor und Gesetz: Zur 'Morphologischen Methode' bei Goethe and Wittgenstein," *Grazer Philosophische Studien* 21 (1984); and G. P. Baker and P. M. S. Hacker, *Wittgenstein: Understanding and Meaning*

(Oxford: Basil Blackwell, 1980), 537–540. I summarize and comment on this work in my *Leading a Human Life: Wittgenstein, Intentionality, and Romanticism* (Chicago: University of Chicago Press, 1997), 177–181.

2. Thomas Mann, "On Goethe's *Werther*," trans. Elizabeth Corra, in *The Sufferings of Young Werther and Elective Affinities*, ed. Victor Lange (New York: Continuum, 1990), 2.

3. Charles Taylor, *Sources of the Self: The Making of the Modern Identity* (Cambridge, Mass.: Harvard University Press, 1989), x.

4. Ibid., 18.

5. Philippe Lacoue-Labarthe and Jean-Luc Nancy, *The Literary Absolute: The Theory of Literature in German Romanticism*, trans. Philip Barnard and Cheryl Lester (Albany: State University of New York Press, 1988), 31.

6. Ibid., 12. The subject term of Lacoue-Labarthe and Nancy's clauses is "literary production," not "articulation," but with the migration of human self-production toward the literary, in a mix of discovery and invention, the latter, more general term makes their characterizations appropriate to human moral efforts in general.

7. Rodolphe Gasché, foreword to Friedrich Schlegel, *Philosophical Fragments*, trans. Peter Firchow (Minneapolis: University of Minnesota Press, 1991), xix.

8. Nicholas Boyle, *Goethe: The Poet and the Age*, vol. 1.: *The Poetry of Desire* (Oxford: Clarendon Press, 1991), 176.

9. Ibid., 124.

10. Ibid., 110.

11. Ibid., 177.

12. Ibid., 162.

13. Ibid., 176.

14. Mann, "On Goethe's *Werther*," 9.

15. Ibid., 9, 10.

16. Johann Wolfgang von Goethe, *The Sorrows of Young Werther*, in *Goethe: The Collected Works*, ed. David E. Wellbery, trans. Victor Lange (Princeton, N.J.: Princeton University Press, 1994), 11:72. Subsequent references to *Werther* will all be to this edition and will be indicated in the text by page number.

17. Mann, "On Goethe's *Werther*," 8.

18. Ray Monk, *Ludwig Wittgenstein: The Duty of Genius* (New York: The Free Press, 1990), 25.

19. Brian McGuinness, *Wittgenstein, A Life: Young Ludwig 1889–1921* (Berkeley: University of California Press, 1988), 156.

20. Ibid., 50.

21. Ibid.

22. Ibid., 156, citing Tolstoy, "A Confession."

23. Ludwig Wittgenstein, *Culture and Value*, trans. Peter Winch (Oxford: Basil Blackwell, 1980), 1e. Subsequent references to this work will be given by page numbers in parentheses.

24. This remark is about "an ordinary conventional figure" at the end of Schubert's "Death and the Maiden," but it captures well Wittgenstein's attitude toward the manual work he repeatedly urged on others.

25. Goethe, *Die Leiden des jungen Werther* (Stuttgart: Reclam, 1948), 147. Werther actually adds one more line to Wilhelm: "wir sehen uns wieder und freudiger" (147). But "Lebt wohl!" alone is what lives in the memory of his readers as his valedictory to life, particularly since his last diary entry, addressed to Lotte, concludes "Es schlägt zwölfe. So sei es denn!—Lotte! Lotte, lebe wohl! lebe wohl!" (150).

26. Wittgenstein, *Philosophical Investigations*, 3rd ed., trans. G. E. M. Anscombe (New York: Macmillan, 1958), §125, pp. 50, 50e. Subsequent references to this work will be given in the text by section number.

27. Wittgenstein, cited in Norman Malcolm, *Ludwig Wittgenstein: A Memoir* (Oxford: Oxford University Press, 1958), 100.

4. Attention, Expressive Power, and Interest in Life: Wordsworth's "Tintern Abbey"

1. Nietzsche, *The Birth of Tragedy and The Case of Wagner*, trans. Walter Kaufmann (New York: Random House, 1967), §1, 33.

2. While some may argue that Jesus is an ideal human being, he is at best ideal as a person and personification, not as 5'2", eyes of blue.

3. Nietzsche, *The Birth of Tragedy*, §14, 91.

4. Nietzsche, *The Will to Power*, trans. Walter Kaufmann (New York: Random House, 1968), 1050.

5. Nietzsche, *The Birth of Tragedy*, §1, 33.

6. Ibid., §7, 59.

7. Ibid., §7, 60.

8. Ibid.

9. Ibid.

10. Ibid., §7, 58.

11. Ibid.

12. Aristotle, *Poetics*, trans. Richard Janko (Indianapolis, Ind.: Hackett Publishing Company, 1987), 51b1, p. 12.

13. For a defense of this reading of Aristotle's account of the nature of the *hamartia* or "tragic flaw" as an excess of virtue ill-suited to the circumstances of action, see Richard Eldridge, "How Can Tragedy Matter for Us?" in Eldridge, *The Persistence of Romanticism* (Cambridge: Cambridge University Press, 2001), 146–164.

14. Nietzsche, *The Birth of Tragedy*, §7, 58.

15. Ibid.

16. William Wordsworth, *The Prelude* [1850], in Wordsworth, *Selected Poems and Prefaces*, ed. Jack Stillinger (Boston: Houghton Mifflin Company, 1965), book 14, ll. 161–162, p. 360.

17. Wordsworth, "From *The Recluse*" [Prospectus], in *Selected Poems and Prefaces*, l. 808, p. 46.

18. On Wordsworth's conjecturalism, see Eldridge, "Internal Transcendentalism: Wordsworth and 'A New Condition of Philosophy,'" in Eldridge, *The Persistence of Romanticism*, 102–123.

19. Wordsworth, *The Prelude*, 1, ll. 267–269, p. 199.

20. Wordsworth, "Preface to the Second Edition of *Lyrical Ballads*," in Wordsworth, *Selected Poems and Prefaces*, 446, 447. Subsequent references to the "Preface" will be given by page number in the text.

21. Stanley Cavell, "The Philosopher in American Life," in Cavell, *In Quest of the Ordinary* (Chicago: The University of Chicago Press,), 7.

22. Cavell, "Emerson, Coleridge, Kant," in Cavell, *In Quest of the Ordinary*, 36. See also Cavell, "Texts of Recovery," 52–53.

23. Cavell, "Being Odd, Getting Even," in Cavell, *In Quest of the Ordinary*, 115–116.

24. Cavell notes the interest of the formulation "communicate with" and its difference from "communicate about" in "Texts of Recovery," 71–72.

25. David E. Wellbery, *The Specular Moment: Goethe's Early Lyric and the Beginnings of Romanticism* (Stanford, Calif.: Stanford University Press, 1996), 39.

26. See ibid., 11.

27. Ibid., 55.

28. Wordsworth, *The Prelude*, 14, ll. 439–443, p. 366.

29. Wordsworth, *Alfoxden Notebook*, 21v, in *The Ruined Cottage and*

the Pedlar, ed. James Butler (Ithaca, N.Y.: Cornell University Press, 1979), 125.

30. David S. Miall, "Locating Wordsworth: 'Tintern Abbey' and the Community with Nature," *Romanticism on the Net* 20 (November 2000), available online at http://www.erudit.org/revue/ron/2000/v/n20/005949ar.html, p. 1.

31. Cavell, "Postscript B: Poe's Perversity and the Imp(ulse) of Skepticism," in Cavell, *In Quest of the Ordinary*, 143.

32. Wordsworth, "Lines Composed a Few Miles Above Tintern Abbey, On Revisiting the Banks of the Wye During a Tour, July 13, 1798," in Wordsworth, *Selected Poems and Prefaces*, 108–111. References to the poem will be to this edition and will be given by line number in the text.

33. David Bromwich, "The French Revolution and 'Tintern Abbey,'" *Raritan* 10, no. 3 (Winter 1991): 1–23.

34. This suggestion is made most notably by Marjorie Levinson in "Insight and Oversight: Reading 'Tintern Abbey,'" in Levinson, *Wordsworth's Great Period Poems* (Cambridge: Cambridge University Press, 1986), 14–57, esp. 37: "the primary poetic action [of 'Tintern Abbey'] is the suppression of the social" in favor of a 'fiercely private vision.'" See also Jerome McGann, *The Romantic Ideology* (Chicago: University of Chicago Press, 1983), 85–88.

35. Miall, "Locating Wordsworth," 3.

36. Wordsworth, *The Prelude*, 2, ll. 277–281, p. 213.

37. For further discussion of this famous sentence from chapter 4 of Hegel's *Phenomenology of Spirit*, trans. A.V. Miller (Oxford: Clarendon Press, 1977), para. 167, p. 105, see Eldridge, *Leading a Human Life: Wittgenstein, Intentionality, and Romanticism* (Chicago: University of Chicago Press, 1997), 27–32.

38. Wordsworth, *The Prelude*, 2, ll. 228–232, p. 212.

39. Bromwich, "The French Revolution and 'Tintern Abbey,'" 8.

40. John Barrell, *Poetry, Language, and Politics* (Manchester: Manchester University Press, 1988), 162.

41. Ibid.

42. I seem to recall having learned this interpretation of "never did" from reading Geoffrey Hartman, but I cannot now locate the reference.

43. John Dewey, "Construction and Criticism," in *Later Works* (Carbondale, Ind.: The Center for Dewey Studies, 1988), 5:125–146. I thank Nikolas Kompridis for directing my attention to this remark.

44. Geoffrey H. Hartman, *Wordsworth's Poetry 1787–1814*, 2nd. ed. (New Haven, Conn.: Yale University Press, 1971), xv.

45. Ibid., 190.

46. Ibid., 104.

47. Ibid.

48. Ibid., 218.

49. Ibid., 38.

5. *The Ends of Literary Narrative: Rilke's "Archaic Torso of Apollo"*

1. Peter Lamarque and Stein Haugom Olsen, *Truth, Fiction, and Literature* (Oxford: The Clarendon Press, 1996), 369–378. Subsequent references to this work will be given in the main text by page numbers in parentheses.

2. Lamarque and Olsen are quoting Theseus, in Shakespeare, *A Midsummer Night's Dream*, act 5, scene 1.

3. John Gibson, "Reality and the Language of Fiction," in *Writing the Austrian Traditions: Themes in Philosophy and Literature*, ed. Wolfgang Huemer and Marc-Oliver Schuster (Toronto: University of Toronto Press, 2003), 63. Subsequent references to this work will be given in the main text by page numbers in parentheses.

4. Gibson takes up these questions in much greater detail, in ways that fill in a story about human life in ways I find congenial, in his *Fiction and the Weave of Life* (Oxford University Press, 2008) and "Literature and Knowledge," in *Oxford Handbook of Philosophy and Literature*, ed. Richard Eldridge (Oxford University Press, forthcoming). Both these pieces develop a version of the working-through conception that I am urging.

5. The cognitive developmental psychologist Michael Tomasello has recently developed a rich account of language learning as depending essentially on intention-reading in his *The Cultural Origins of Human Cognition* (Cambridge, Mass.: Harvard University Press, 1999) and *Constructing a Language: A Usage-Based Theory of Language Acquisition* (Cambridge, Mass.: Harvard University Press, 2003). His account builds in part on Wittgenstein's work on seeing-as in part 2 of *Philosophical Investigations*, 3rd. ed., trans. G. E. M. Anscombe (New York: Macmillan, 1958). I survey the affinities between the views of Tomasello and Wittgenstein in "Wittgenstein on Aspect-Seeing, the Nature of Discursive Consciousness, and

the Experience of Agency," in *Seeing Wittgenstein Anew: New Essays on Aspect-Seeing*, ed. William Day and Victor Krebs (Cambridge: Cambridge University Press, forthcoming). R. G. Collingwood treats language learning and concept learning in similar terms, as a matter of learning by interacting with others and how to attend to aspects, in Collingwood, *The Principles of Art* (Oxford: The Clarendon Press, 1938), esp. 239–241.

6. I take the idea that language *must* be both *stable* in providing us with ways of thinking of things that we use internally and unhesitatingly and *tolerant* of new usages from Stanley Cavell, *The Claim of Reason* (New York: Oxford University Press, 1979), 185–186.

7. I take up the essential "immigrancy" involved in our inheritance of language and development of conceptual consciousness in "Cavell and Hölderlin on Human Immigrancy," in Eldridge, *The Persistence of Romanticism* (Cambridge: Cambridge University Press, 2001), 229–245.

8. Collingwood, *The Principles of Art*, 239. Collingwood is almost surely thinking here also of Freud's account of the development of the ego in and through plays of mutual attention and contestation. See Freud on the *fort-da* game in Freud, *Beyond the Pleasure Principle*, trans. James Strachey (New York: Bantam Books, 1961).

9. See Spinoza, Benedict de, *Ethics*, in Spinoza, *Selections*, ed. John Wild (New York: Charles Scribner's Sons, 1930), part 5, propositions 3–10, pp. 369–377.

10. Cavell develops his account of the truth of skepticism in various major writings, including "Knowing and Acknowledging" (1969), *The Claim of Reason* (1979), "Being Odd, Getting Even" (1986), and *Conditions Handsome and Unhandsome* (1990). For an overview of Cavell's thoughts about skepticism, see Richard Eldridge, "'A Continuing Task': Cavell and the Truth of Skepticism," in Eldridge, *The Persistence of Romanticism*, 189–204.

11. Charles Altieri, *The Particulars of Rapture: An Aesthetics of the Affects* (Ithaca, N.Y.: Cornell University Press, 2003), 107.

12. William Wordsworth, "Preface to *Lyrical Ballads*," in *Selected Poems and Prefaces*, ed. Jack Stillinger (Boston: Houghton Mifflin Company, 1965), 448.

13. See Friedrich Hölderlin, "On Religion," in Hölderlin, *Essays and Letters on Theory*, trans. and ed. Thomas Pfau (Albany: State University of New York Press, 1988), 90–91.

14. John Dewey, *Art as Experience* (New York: Penguin, 1980), esp. chapter 3, "Having an Experience," and 17–19.

15. See Richard Eldridge, *Leading a Human Life: Wittgenstein, Intentionality, and Romanticism* (Chicago: University of Chicago Press, 1997), 6–7; *The Persistence of Romanticism*, 19–20, 55–57, 158–163, 235; and *An Introduction to the Philosophy of Art* (Cambridge: Cambridge University Press, 2003), 7–12, 262.

16. Barbara Herrnstein Smith, *Poetic Closure: A Study of How Poems End* (Chicago: University of Chicago Press, 1968), 36. Subsequent references to this work will be given in the main text by page numbers in parentheses.

17. See Friedrich Nietzsche, *The Use and Abuse of History*, trans. Adrian Collins (Indianapolis, Ind.: The Bobbs-Merrill Company, 1949), 5.

18. Friedrich Nietzsche, "'Reason' in Philosophy," trans. Walter Kaufmann, in Nietzsche, *The Twilight of the Idols*, excerpted in *The Portable Nietzsche*, ed. Walter Kaufmann (New York: The Viking Press, 1954), 479.

19. Friedrich Nietzsche, *The Birth of Tragedy and The Case of Wagner*, trans. Walter Kaufmann (New York: Random House, 1967), 59. In *The Aesthetic Dimension*, Marcuse argues that "aesthetic affirmation" in life that is not a matter of escapist fantasizing must include a sense of the ontologically "irreconcilable" and that it is expressed aptly in the last words of the "Song of the Tower Warden" in Goethe's *Faust*: "Es war doch so schön." Herbert Marcuse, *The Aesthetic Dimension*, trans. Herbert Marcuse and Erica Sherover (Boston: Beacon Press, 1978), 59. See also the concluding discussion of gratitude as a response to the experience of the truth of skepticism in Eldridge, *Leading a Human Life*, 286–290.

20. Friedrich Nietzsche, *Writings from the Late Notebook*, ed. Rüdiger Bittner (Cambridge: Cambridge University Press, 2003), 159–160.

21. Steven Winn, "Endings Are a Catharsis," *San Francisco Chronicle*, January 1, 2005. Available online at http://sfgate.com/cgi-bin/article. cgi?file=/chronicle/archive/2005/01/01/DDG7VAJAL81.DTL.

22. Frank Kermode, *The Sense of an Ending: Studies in the Theory of Fiction, with a New Epilogue* (Oxford: Oxford University Press, 2000), 138. Subsequent references to this work will be given in the main text by page numbers in parentheses.

23. Judith Ryan, *Rilke, Modernism, and Poetic Tradition* (Cambridge: Cambridge University Press, 1999), 82.

24. Ibid., 89.
25. Ibid., 98.
26. Ibid., 83–84.
27. Rainer Maria Rilke, *The Selected Poetry of Rainer Maria Rilke*, ed. and trans. Stephen Mitchell (New York: Random House, 1982), 60–61.
28. Ryan, *Rilke, Modernism, and Poetic Tradition*, 36.
29. Ibid., 83.
30. Ibid., 84.
31. Ibid., 86.

6. *"New Centers of Reflection Are Continually Forming":* *Benjamin, Sebald, and Modern Human Life in Time*

1. The quotation that forms the title of this chapter is from Walter Benjamin, "The Concept of Criticism in German Romanticism," trans. David Lachterman, Howard Eiland, and Ian Balfour, in Benjamin, *Selected Writings, Volume 1: 1913–1926*, ed. Marcus Bullock and Michael W. Jennings (Cambridge, Mass.: Harvard University Press, 1996), 156.

2. G.W.F. Hegel, *Aesthetics: Lectures on Fine Art*, trans. T.M. Knox (Oxford: Clarendon Press, 1975), 31.

3. Hegel, *Phenomenology of Spirit*, trans. A.V. Miller (Oxford: Clarendon Press, 1977), para. 32, p. 19.

4. An attentive reader for Columbia University Press urged this formulation on me.

5. Stephen Houlgate, "Introduction: An Overview of Hegel's Aesthetics," in *Hegel and the Arts*, ed. Stephen Houlgate (Evanston, Ill.: Northwestern University Press, 2007), xxv.

6. Terry Pinkard, "Symbolic, Classical, and Romantic Art," in *Hegel and the Arts*, 5.

7. G. W. F. Hegel, *Lectures on Fine Art*, trans. T. M. Knox (Oxford: The Clarendon Press, 1975), 1:97.

8. Ibid., 98.

9. Hegel, *Elements of the Philosophy of Right*, trans. H.B. Nisbet (Cambridge: Cambridge University Press, 1991), 14.

10. In emphasizing the "good-enough" reconciliation theme in Hegel, I have been influenced by Michael O. Hardimon, *Hegel's Social Philosophy: The Project of Reconciliation* (Cambridge: Cambridge University Press, 1994).

11. Walter Benjamin, "On Language as Such," trans. Rodney Livingstone, in Benjamin, *Selected Writings: Volume 1, 1913–1926*, 73, 70.

12. Ibid., 73.

13. See Donald Davidson's classic "On the Very Idea of a Conceptual Scheme" and "The Method of Truth in Metaphysics," both in Davidson, *Inquiries Into Truth and Interpretation* (Oxford: Clarendon Press, 1984), for an argument to this effect. For a commentary on the powers but also on the limits of this argument, specifically how it leaves specifically problems of practical engagement between subjects unaddressed, see Alasdair MacIntyre, "Relativism, Power, and Philosophy," in *After Philosophy: End or Transformation?*, ed. Kenneth Baynes, James Bohman, and Thomas McCarthy (Cambridge, Mass.: The MIT Press, 1987), and Richard Eldridge, "Metaphysics and the Interpretation of Persons: Davidson on Thinking and Conceptual Schemes," *Synthese* 66, no. 3 (March 1986): 477–503.

14. Benjamin, "On Language as Such," 66.

15. Michael Rosen, "Benjamin, Adorno, and the Decline of the Aura," in *The Cambridge Companion to Critical Theory*, ed. Fred Rush (Cambridge: Cambridge University Press, 2004), 46.

16. Benjamin, *The Arcades Project*, trans. H. Eiland and K. McLaughlin (Cambridge, Mass.: Harvard University Press, 1999), 460.

17. Anthony Lane, "Higher Ground: Adventures in Fact and Fiction from W. G. Sebald," *The New Yorker*, May 29, 2000.

18. Susan Sontag, *Where the Stress Falls* (New York: Farrar, Straus and Giroux, 2001), 41.

19. Ibid., 46, 48, 46.

20. Franz Loquai, "Vom Beinhaus der Geschichte ins wiedergefundene Paradies: Zu Werk und Poetik W. G. Sebalds," in *Sebald. Lektüren*, ed. Marcel Atze and Franz Loquai (Eggingen: Edition Isele, 2005), 244. My translation.

21. See Farrell, *Why Does Literature Matter?*, 199.

22. Ibid., 197.

23. Ibid., 200.

24. Mark R. McCulloh, *Understanding W. G. Sebald* (Columbia: University of South Carolina Press, 2003), 19.

25. W. G. Sebald, *Der Mythus der Zerstörung im Werk Döblins* (Stuttgart: Klett, 1980), 58; cited in McCulloh, *Understanding W. G. Sebald*, 148. McCulloh's translation.

26. Eric L. Santner, *On Creaturely Life* (Chicago: University of Chicago Press, 2006), 49.

27. Ibid., 114, n. 20.

28. Ibid., 20.

29. Ibid.

30. Ibid., 71.

31. Ibid., 74.

32. Ibid., 81, 84; in the latter passage Santner is drawing on Alenka Zupancic, *The Shortest Shadow: Nietzsche's Philosophy of the Two* (Cambridge, Mass.: The MIT Press, 2003), 49.

33. Wordsworth, *The Prelude* (1850), book 7, ll. 725–728, p. 288.

34. Hegel, *Elements of the Philosophy of Right*, para. 185, p. 222.

35. Santner, *On Creaturely Life*, 134.

36. Ibid., 133.

37. Ibid., 136, citing Jonathan Lear, *Happiness, Death, and the Remainder of Life* (Cambridge, Mass.: Harvard University Press, 2000), 129.

38. Ibid., 203.

39. Terry Eagleton, *Walter Benjamin, or Towards a Revolutionary Criticism* (London: Verson, 1985), 42; cited in Santner, *On Creaturely Life*, 134, n. 54.

40. Santner, *On Creaturely Life*, 75.

41. Ibid.

42. Ibid., 81.

43. Walter Benjamin, "Surrealism," trans. Rodney Livingstone, in Benjamin, *Selected Writings: Volume 2, 1927–1934*, ed. Michael W. Jennings, Howard Eiland, and Gary Smith (Cambridge, Mass.: Harvard University Press, 1999), 216. Sebald cites this passage in *Die Beschreibung des Unglücks: Zur österreichischen Literatur von Stifter bis Handke* (Frankfurt am Main: Fisscher, 1994), 132. McCulloh, *Understanding W.G. Sebald*, 155, n. 11, notes this citation.

44. McCulloh, *Understanding W.G. Sebald*, 3.

45. Walter Benjamin, "The Concept of Criticism in German Romanticism," in Benjamin, *Selected Writings, Volume 1: 1913–1926*, 116–200. All references to this work will be given by page number in the text.

46. In the opening lines of his *The Origin of German Tragic Drama*, Benjamin remarks that "it is characteristic of philosophical writing that at every turn it must confront the question of representation [*Darstellung*] anew." On the significance of this remark, see Azade Seyhan, *Representation and*

Its Discontents: The Critical Legacy of German Romanticism (Berkeley: University of California Press, 1992); and Martha B. Helfer, *The Retreat of Representation: The Concept of Darstellung in German Critical Discourse* (Albany: State University of New York Press, 1996).

47. Herbert Marcuse, *The Aesthetic Dimension*, trans. Herbert Marcuse and Erica Sherover (Boston: Beacon Press, 1978), 59.

48. See also the slightly different translation in Friedrich Schlegel, "On Goethe's *Meister*," trans. Joyce Crick, in *Classical and Romantic German Aesthetics*, ed. J. M. Bernstein (Cambridge: Cambridge University Press, 2003), 273.

49. W. G. Sebald, "Paul Bereyter," in *The Emigrants*, trans. Michael Hulse (London: Vintage, 2002), 25–63; W. G. Sebald, "Paul Bereyter," in *Die Ausgewanderten: Vier lange Erzählungen* (Frankfurt am Main: Fischer, 1994), 39–93. Citations to these works will be given in the text by English page number followed by German page number.

50. "Manchem göttliche Gemüte wird vom Schicksal eine unförmliche Form aufgedrungen, wie dem Sokrates der Satyr-Leib; denn über die Form, nicht über den innern Stoff regiert die Zeit. So hing der poetische Spiegel, womit Jakob Böhme Himmel und Erde wiedergibt, in einem dunklen Orte; auch mangelt dem Glase an einigen Stellen die Folie. So ist der große Hamann ein tiefer Himmel voll teleskopischer Sterne, und manche Nebelflecken löset kein Auge auf." Jean Paul, *Vorschule der Ästhetik*, in *Sämtliche Werke*, vol. 3 (Paris, 1836–1837); English translation in Jean Paul Richter, *Horn of Oberon*, trans. Margaret R. Hale, (Detroit, Mich.: Wayne State University Press, 1973), 41–42.

51. Dante, *The Divine Comedy I: Hell*, trans. Dorothy Sayers (Harmondsworth: Penguin, 1949), canto 1, ll. 1–3, p. 71.

Index

absorption, 6–7, 9
Adorno, T. W., 11, 16–17, 47
Althusser, Louis, 123
Altieri, Charles, 19, 109
Appelo, Tim, 45
Aristotle, 11, 15, 21, 73, 113
Austen, Jane, 9, 43
Austin, J. L., 24, 44, 159n25
autopoiesis, 52

Baker, Gordon, 49
Banville, Theodore de, 115, 117
Barrell, John, 25, 95–96
Baudelaire, Charles, 8–9, 117
Beckett, Samuel, 42–43, 163n45
Benjamin, Walter, 124–27
Bentham, Jeremy, 102
Bernstein, Charles, 22
Bernstein, J. M., 8–9
Blake, William, 34, 39
Bloom, Harold, 42
Booth, Wayne, 157n2
Bourdieu, Pierre, 25
Boyle, Nicholas, 53–55
Bromwich, David, 92, 167n33
Brown, Dan, 103
Byron, Lord (Baron George Gordon), 38–39
Byronism, 38–43, 46

Cartesianism, 36–38, 39–43, 46, 110, 112
catharsis, 61, 119
Cavell, Stanley, 13–14, 76, 79, 80–81, 84, 109, 169n6
childhood, 5, 11, 143–44, 147
close reading, 2, 24–25
closure, aesthetic, 6–7, 20,110–11, 113, 137–38
Cohen, Ted, 161n52
Collingwood, R. G., 108, 169n5
consciousness, conceptual, 10–12, 15–16, 91, 96, 98–99, 107–8
Coolidge, Clark, 22
curricula, literary, 1–3

Dante (Alighieri), 149
Davidson, Donald, 172n13
depression, 30, 50–51, 53, 83
Descartes, René, 12–13, 28, 32, 36–38
desire, 15, 55, 92
Dewey, John, 11, 27–30, 32, 36, 98, 109
didacticism, 20
disruption, aesthetic, 5–7, 23
Döblin, Alfred, 129
Don Giovanni, 39
Don Quixote, 9